THE TIME

How To Time Your Actions To Turn Challenges Into Opportunities

Ysanne Lewis

www.ysanne.com

Date first Published: 21 December 2016, London

Published by RADIO W.O.R.K.S. WORLD
www.RadioWorks.World

ISBN 978-0-9534507-1-8

To Mark 12/2/19
warmly
Ysanne

For YOU,
The lovers of life's mysteries
and your friends
who are curious
to know more!

Ysanne

Contents

From the Author's desk, YSANNE LEWIS

MY STORY ABOUT

THE TIME CATCHER

Welcome to this book!

It is such a pleasure to write on a subject we all live with and do our best to align with: The Mystery of Time.
I have often been asked by people to create a book on how I view the subject, and to pull together strands of thought, research and discoveries on the cycles and pages from the 'book of life' which is there just waiting to be read.
I anticipate my writing will stimulate more questions than answers and I actually hope that is the case. It is how it should be as we grow and expand like the universe does.

'Doing time' on this planet that we live on, we travel with it as a silent but obvious companion. We keep saying that time is going *so* fast. Maybe we need a new relationship with it? The year of 2016 was unpredictable and uncertain for many of us and it is easy to feel 'off kilter'. Recognising we are part of a bigger picture and finding some ways to make sense of the passage of time needs a fresh look at the beautiful world around us, which contains all the information we need to be more in harmony with proportion, time and space.

I wrote these chapters to remind and encourage us to observe and connect with the natural, seemingly magical patterns, cycles and messages, that are all around us, above, below and within.

Through my decades of working as a timing navigator, helping people find their way through the twists and turns of life, I have

grown increasingly in awe at how our inner timekeepers know the keys and cycles to working with change and opportunity.
So much in our modern world gets in the way of that though, and I felt this was the right time to take another look.

This isn't, nor do I wish it to be, a specialist book, but an exploration.

Sparking the curiosity and enthusiasm in how we can become more in time and tune with the rhythms that are around us is the thread here. Sensing the threads in nature, the heavens and our bodies, which great minds in the past have been so aware of, is what I would like to encourage in you. Let us glimpse the wonderful intelligence and meaningfulness of this universe.
Over the decades of my life exploring much of this planet, which included my love of the *'embroidered cloths'* of the heavens and nature's tapestry, I have had a passion to make an ancient but timeless subject accessible and relevant to our day to day lives.
Sharing that passion, and what I have explored, is what I offer here.
Time doesn't stand still so let's keep exploring!

I would like to extend a very grateful thank you to my sisters Jeannie and Chrissi for their support. Also to Jenny Nockolds and to Peter Ford for their advice and skills, as *The Time Catcher* came to life.
To Marina Nani, of Radio Works World, who opened this door for me at just the right time, and steered my timing: A big thank you Marina!
And to Andy Schmidt of Santa Barbara, California, who gave kind permission for me to use his lovely photo on the cover.

I also send much appreciation to my friends and to my family of clients worldwide, from over nearly four decades, who have validated and made me so aware of the significance of the beauty and usefulness of good timing in our personal and business life.

FOREWORD
By
Marina Nani

Are you an Explorer at heart?

The greatest adventures known in human history start within the front and back cover of a book. There is a whole new world within, like a new planet of big ideas and original versions of a refreshing, better reality. Those brave enough to go on an adventure and step in, even out of disbelief or just curiosity, could become part of a new generation of explorers, and even in our cyber times I like to call them 'Columbus'. If you are an explorer, a Columbus at heart, this book is for you.

What resonates with you, vibrates within, and I found Ysanne's book to be not only profound in its unique beauty but filled with messages that help you time your actions to turn challenges into opportunities. There are no coincidences, if you are reading this book, it means you were seeking for inner guidance to endorse your own vision.
Ysanne Lewis's book gives you an appetite for spiralling outside your 'common sky' into the unknown, making the longest journey you will ever take; the 18 inches distance between your heart and your mind - your playground.

Being ahead of times is a secret desire that is hard to resist. Who wouldn't want to know what's next? When you feel trapped or left outside in the cold, the first thing that comes to mind is "if I only knew then what I know now". What happens between "then" and "now" is very much a consequence of living your life with the end in mind. Being ahead of yourself, even by two steps, gives you an unfair advantage.

Ysanne's book gives you the tools to think ahead and engage with your future and the power of your intentions. Ysanne helps you align your actions, beliefs and values with your emotions, and turn your inner vision into reality. What you could experience being guided by Ysanne is not only positioning yourself under your lucky stars, but becoming one.

I truly enjoyed this exceptional book, which is mirroring Ysanne's show on our radio station where, together with hundreds of story tellers from around the world, she is generously sharing her own passion. Remember, the same way the moon has no light of her own, but an extraordinary power of reflection, this book's successful adventure depends on your ability to reflect on its powerful message and take it to your heart. Don't rush; as Ysanne says "Time is on your side".

Marina Nani, Author, Founder, Radio W.O.R.K.S. World

Chapter One

THE ART OF TIMING

"But he who kisses the joy as it flies lives in eternity's sunrise"

William Blake

The art of timing lives within us. To grow gracefully with time we need to form a relationship with it as we would a person, project, or even a piece of music. Growing gracefully with any art or relationship makes necessary an understanding of the ebb and the rising tide, as well as the occasional seventh ocean wave – the big one.

'Time', even though apparently topping the list in June 2016 in the Oxford English Dictionary as the most popular and most used noun (they update every seasonal quarter of the year), is something we have quite a careless relationship with, let alone a sufficient respect for.

Being on time is one thing, as is following clock time and appointments and calendars, but what about the framework for our natural diaries, which are more invisible and can be at odds with the former?

We can all be timing experts by adopting certain awarenesses and mindfulness skills and it is simpler than it seems.

So how did I develop a relationship with timing and come to embrace it? How can *you*? Like many of us the cliches about time surrounded me over the years. Expressions such as: *"Time flies,"*

"in the nick of time", "out of time", "borrowed time" and endless quotes from poetry and plays, e.g: *"Time's winged chariot."*
'Feeling between time zones' as an expression of emotional confusion, is a modern way of looking at how lost and disoriented we can be in our lives when we are not in touch with our inner navigator or fully present in time.

As a child I was fascinated by the upside down carpet of the skies and nature's ever changing seasons and beautiful clothing styles! I devoured myths and stories of star lore, not realising at that young age that in times past our ancestors were very aware of how those stories they projected onto the skies held a deep resonance in humanity's psyche. Even in our present times they continue being lived out in day to day life, politics and relationships.

My love of patterns, myths, numbers and the timing of cycles began to form a cohesive picture from the jigsaw pieces when I chose to explore astrology (*astro-star and logos-word*) not realising then that I would make it a good friend and my vocation for the rest of my life. Time has shown me that planetary cycles have their regularity, intertwining with our own lives and business projects. Everything has a birth chart, a starting point, with resultant troughs and peaks.

Curiosity has always accompanied me and I have never been bored with the exploration of the connections between what is above and what is below. Some of this I am looking forward to sharing with you!

Playing a part in acting as a bridge and navigator between the messages in nature, the cosmos, our inner timekeepers and the cycles set in motion at our birth times, humbles me. I realise that the beautiful intelligence at work in the universal mind and how it guides us to cooperate and make sense of change is present.

I recall reading how the physicist James Jeans once talked about how the universe is becoming more and more like a great mind, rather than a great machine.

If we allow ourselves to see how the movements of the planets correlate with life here on Earth, how can we not see the connectedness of everything? We can stop feeling isolated or lonely when we feel and relate to the planetary cycles and nature's rhythms. In bodies, even though our souls may be from elsewhere, we are creatures of cycles; to be in health helps to recognise that. When we step out of step with these alignments we reinforce the sense of separation and poor timing.

We all know how a false start disturbs the race or dance. Throughout this book I will be addressing ways to cooperate with the inner and outer tides, bringing us home to ourselves in ways that our ancient and modern minds intrinsically remember at their heart.
We are living in a time of accelerated change. Hopefully, it is accelerated growth of the good type. More and more we hear the complaint that time is going faster. And, like with the seventh big wave seen in the ocean's movement, things can happen more rapidly in a week in politics than in a decade! I am thinking here of the referendum in the UK in June 2016 and the amount of changes of leadership, stepping down and ascending into positions of power that occurred.

In our three dimensional world aren't we part of, and bound to, space and time? Without our bodies we would not be. So, maybe do *we* influence time and how we subjectively experience it?
It is part of our human condition to believe and work with linear time. Quantum physics says that perhaps time past, present and future, may all be happening at once, but to keep our sanity we experience time as sequential through the filters of the brain and senses. We can use it to help us choose start up times and balance our energy flow for health and choices.

Our ancestors had this timing skill down to quite a fine art. Yes, of course life has nowadays presented us with multiple choices and a more controlled technological environment, as well as the stresses born out of many factors, but our forbears relied more on the rituals of the natural year. They recognised the interconnectedness of life and they didn't need the sophisticated science and instruments we have now to have a reasonable understanding of astronomy. The right timings would be chosen astronomically for major festivals, coronations, royal marriages, wars and the like. The fast and slow variations in the sky's appearance helped civilizations keep track of time as a navigational aid. They were signposts and markers for change and acknowledgement.

We have many, many more options now. However, although we have more sophisticated aids for tracking and navigation, the inner terrain map can also keep us on track. *'As without so within'*.

Indeed, we are all natural astrologers at heart just as we are part of the solar system and sense its resonance unconsciously. We say “nature knows best” or “mother knows best”, without perhaps being aware that the word nature means ‘that which is born' and links with the word *natal*. The *Moon* links with the words *mother* and *matter*.

Yet we are the only species who generally don't obey our diurnal cycles....

A COMMON SKY

We live under a common sky physically. The earth beneath us and the sky above us are saturated with rhythms and a quiet patience which we can choose to cooperate with or impose our will on. We are strung between heaven and earth, with the task of being spiritual beings in human bodies and understanding with compassion what it is to be human. We are both of star dust and of the earth. There is a natural dance, an interplay of ecstasy and creativity, yet we often make our being a battleground via the tools of rigid religion, mistrust and the tension born of fear and control. Fear and control are two sides of the same coin.

Time and again I work with clients who can relate to the cycles of the time ebbs and flows I see mirrored in their birth charts. This is because these cycles are *in us*, set into motion when we are born. What we do with them with our freewill is up to us, but at least knowing their timings gives a certain advantage when faced with choices and doubts. This language is a way to interpret cycles of growth, large and small rhythms of time, cells within cells.
At the moment of the birth of a person, project, country or event, the energies of the cosmos touch Earth - a marriage - and hopefully a

strong, not false start! Interestingly, the word '*disaster*' means loss of a star or no star, and '*catastrophe'*, the fall of a star.

We wouldn't set out on a journey by road or sea without some kind of map or timetable of tides would we? We would check the weather, the tides or geographical layout. So, maybe it is only common sense to have some kind of inner sat nav or up to date map. Regular updating is useful too.

It is a good beginning to recognise what isn't in time or flowing right. I am a great believer in the power and guidance of things like auspices, synchronicities and signs from nature; the latter including our bodies of course. Frequency of tiredness, toxicity and confusion can indicate being stuck in old mindsets. When things keep repeating something is telling us we need to change.
Good change occurs when we can release the past with grace, else changes that we don't want can be seemingly forced on us when we are not changing course inside. We are not meant to stand still for long but our minds don't always heed this!

Change is the rule of life but we can fossilize inside by repeating the dialogue of old stories to ourselves.

Conversely, when lovely synchronistic happenings keep popping up, the right help magically appears and things fall into place without our trying. We have somehow, quite beautifully, *got out of our own way.* We have let nature and our higher self guide us rather than the old self born from programmings we have held onto and not up dated.

The outside world will often send us signs we can't ignore, whether from nature or words in a book we open at random. Tribal people have always seen the sacred in portents, signs and symbols, and that language holds true for now. Maybe even more now as we live through uncertain times when many fractured situations and divisions present themselves to our startled eyes.

MEANINGFUL COINCIDENCE

Carl Jung, the great Swiss psychologist, coined the word synchronicity. He described it as meaningful coincidence. A message endorsing a process or route we are on comes our way.
When did you last experience that and what was the feeling it generated?

The fundamental law of resonance means that everything that vibrates acts upon everything else depending upon the vibrational tone. When above moves, what is below cannot fail to move also and, as we are part of the large cell of the solar system, it can be a lovely knowledge to carry within us especially when we feel alone or question the purpose of things and life.
It has been said that what is ours comes to us. With vibration that is certainly true. In a later chapter when I write about numbers and cycles I will cover this more, but for now let's give a thought to the threads that connect us all and how we can weave our way to resonate with the right ones at the right times. Remember what I mentioned earlier that all the mapping and signals live within us, and we don't need to be birds or other of nature's creatures to have this instinct. In fact, observing how the wild life we see around us daily operate can give us healthy clues and a reminder that our bodies are part of nature too. It's a good start anyway!

We don't need to act like our far off ancestors who created rituals to make sure the sun rose again in the morning. But we can still choose to experience that moment or two before it does. We sense the earth almost holding its breath, and the stillness before the life giving Sun appears over the eastern horizon. Even churches, in the main, faced east when they were built.

The ancient Greeks related in their myths the lovely story of the god Charon, the ferryman, who carried the souls of the dead across the river Styx to the underworld, popping the Sun in the back of his boat in the evening and letting it out again in the east in the morning! A nice allegory. The imagination is a fantastic way of making connections.

And the genius scientist that Albert Einstein was wrote that, "***The power of the imagination is the ultimate creative power...no doubt about that. While knowledge defines all we currently know and understand...imagination points to all we might yet discover and create. Imagination is more important than knowledge. Your imagination is your preview of life's coming attractions.***"

Way back in the 2nd century AD, Ptolemy described the planets as lively gods within us, saying that the sky within, our inner geography, was as vast as the sky without. Astronomy was the first science, star lore the first religion, and it is remarkable how they are so relevant to making sense and giving meaning to modern life.

SPIRALS OF GROWTH

Sometimes we miss our cue and miss an opportunity, but that's part of clock time. There is always another cycle, a turn of the wheel, to catch our timing better next time. Spirals permeate life from within, from the DNA, to plants, to star nebulae, the Milky Way and in many man made structures. Not just circular, but rising to the next level. Visualize this when you feel trapped or in a kind of ground hog day situation. Spirals denote eternity in the sense they go on forever and symbolise the longing for and growth towards wholeness.

If life is a path through time, time is curved along with space. It is not just straight. Geometry is the measurement of spatial order and contains beautiful ratios, intervals and relationships. From the material world to the subatomic, all forms are envelopes for geometric patterns. This is truly fascinating.

Kepler and Plato wrote that, "*in the beginning God geometrised.*" This is taking on increasing meaning with what is visible through microscopes and telescopes. The 18th century poet and theorist, Novalis, along with Goethe, talked about all '*form being frozen music*'. Sayings like this open our eyes to the wonderful intelligence in our cosmos. Incidentally, the word cosmos means 'order'.

As we have an imprint of the cosmos within us from when we were born, this makes it possible for astrologers to see, via an ephemeris, when the outer planets in their circuits angle into and return to the positions of the planets when we were born...or our business or consultancy was born.

The art of Timing is woven into the fabric of all these things. Some of us have a heightened awareness and relationship with it. Ranging from clever investors, people who play the stock market, to dancers, musicians and gymnasts, we admire those who slot into timing in what seems with ease.

We all have times when we ride the waves of timing and seize the moment with style! We also have frustrating times when nothing seems to shift or we don't feel comfortable with our bodies or our projects.

With the latter I often liken it to a crossroad, where ideally we should stop, look and listen, else getting locked in or hurt by approaching traffic.

Usually, we know to do the former and all is well, even though we may have to be patient. In our personal life though, we feel the wait will never change. We don't trust the 'gap' in time will fill up again or appreciate and benefit from the pause. And yet a pause is vital for any form of communication with life and people.

TRUST

Trust is an important part of timing. If trapeze artists don't trust that their partners will catch them at just the right second, to use a scary example, a mismatch of timing can result in yes, well.... problems!

On a day to day level it serves us to firstly feel comfortable with our bodies which tell us so much, and then build a good rapport with trusting our instincts. It is so easy to follow the outer world's opinions and advice. Maybe they are right, but sometimes they are not. It's a bit like using a wonky sat nav, GPS or old map, or asking someone the way who means well but misdirects us. We have to stop, pause, and get our own bearings.

In our journey through life our inner compass is trustworthy, but we need to get to know it and feel it orientating us. Like anything this can be cultivated and polished up. Just intending it is a powerful start, otherwise we are forever looking outside for answers to our questions about change and decisions making. How many of us are encouraged that way?
It is very empowering when we quieten the left brain action and trust the deeper signals. Maybe it is a good habit to employ everyday in

small matters so the big ones are easier to trust when they rear their heads!

Impulsiveness is different to spontaneity. This is important to know. Spontaneity springs from being in the moment without too many agendas or impatience, whereas impulsiveness can easily spring from a sense of urgency and being off balance with a thought, spoken word or emotion. Sometimes it is hard to know the difference but the results speak for themselves.

Like any art and skill we can so easily learn to trust and work with our inner timing. We are born with it. Have we forgotten it, like so many other things from childhood knowingness?

Knowing the rhythms of when to do and not do, to initiate and when to wait, when to shed old layers, which our bodies give us plenty of warning signals about, make life so much simpler. This is whether our lives are busy, complicated or relatively simple. The saying, *'There is a time for every season under heaven"*, is so very true.

Let's explore further.

NOTES FOR YOURSELF

Chapter Two

INNER TIMEKEEPERS

"Time is nature's way of keeping everything from happening at once"

John Wheeler, physicist

That quote about time is from a visionary physicist who coined the term black holes and debated relativity theories with Einstein. I love how physics and the imagination are intertwined. It makes us think! At the level of higher mathematics maybe a new realm is entered, where beauty and the bigger web are evident. Einstein and others thought so, so who am I to not agree?

How do you rate your timing? I don't expect you get asked that very much! But, as we have seen from the last chapter, just maybe it plays a significant part in your life and could do with some tweaking.

Are you good at clock time and do appointments flow well as a result?
Are you one of those who like to be early, just in case?
Or do you enjoy the sense of not rushing but ambling up just in time?
Different strokes for different folks.

We all have rhythms wherein we have comfort zones, including being a lark or owl; an early starter to the day or late night bird. There is something to the theory that if you are born near dawn you like the early morning light, and later in the day birth people become more energised as the day goes on. Being born at lunchtime it is still my favourite meal of the day and I look forward to getting truly up to speed later morning. It is one of the reasons I chose to go self employed with a profession which gives me flexibility. Meaning? I can work late at night, writing or talking with clients in different time zones.

Thinking of time zones, I mentioned earlier that occasionally we can feel lost between them. We all know what jet lag can be like. The body feels the bruising, not just of being out of alignment with our normal clock time, but with the effect of hurtling through space; a bruise indeed. This is a different kind of time estrangement.

Time zones define boundaries and are observed for legal, commercial and societal purposes. When travelling, I find it takes a day to make up for an hour difference in time, though it helps to get immediately onto the time zone in question. However, we are all different in how we handle it, just as we are unique in how we walk with time.

Does the start of an activity, conversation or venture lack energy and balance? Or, is it full of presence leading the way into flow and engagement? We don't have to make a performance out of it, but we can in a gentle way be aware of the moment we start something. What are the conditions surrounding it like? How are we feeling?

Have you considered that there is a third energy present; the invisible but connecting power of intention and the 'bringing of yourself to the table'? Any beginning is quite vulnerable yet full of potential and makes its mark with that starting point, its success dependent on the rhythm set into motion. An example is the registration of a company, small business or event. Knowing, or at least sensing, the timing of any of the latter gives us a unique advantage. To quote Carl Jung again, *"Whatever is born at a particular moment in time takes on the quality of that moment"*.

Any actor, dancer, musician knows the importance of the 'beginning', yet, in everyday life, we quite carelessly jump into statements, decisions, perhaps doing too many things at once and ending up wondering how we get into muddles and misunderstandings with others. Techniques linked with dance and music can go a long way to helping us feel and tune in to the right moment for initiating and reaching out. Simple exercises can be learnt to enable this.

Taking a moment to inwardly check if it feels right to engage in something, speak first or even wisely retreat, can be timely! Yes, even timely retreat can be a courageous move of strategy that lends strength to when the time is actually right for us to make a move.

The pauses in music, for example, are powerful ingredients to absorb and to bodily feel at one with the motifs and sentiment of the piece.

STRANGELY GUIDED

When we are not afraid of the spaces and silences, timing has a greater say in our lives and we find that, strangely, we are being guided to the right circumstances, encounter or idea. We wonder, just how did that happen? When there are no gaps or pauses in our busy schedules there is literally no space for magic and the unexpected serendipities. All gets done better when paced or even when we let go of the attachment to it.
A client once told me the inner meaning, of smog!
S.M.O.G: Should, Must, Ought to and Got to. Yes, *smog*... I smiled.

Our inner timekeepers really don't get on with those six words belonging to a smog filled mind.
Yes of course there are responsibilities to fulfil daily, and instead of smog words if we can do our duties with grace and mindfulness, they don't feel so much like chores. Take a couple of examples from your day and try it!

By trying to force the tempo, the natural creative process is blocked. Being in time, whether with dance, music or our daily routine, becomes more effortless and happily received or observed by others when we are in the experience and are *being* the experience.

We say we lose time when lost in a heightened state of enjoyment or a day dream. It can feel like just a minute has passed or maybe a long while has. When we look at the clock afterwards we are surprised at which it is! We are temporarily outside of time.

Stepping outside for a break can be important, not just in work routines but inwardly for self-perspective and soul rest.

THE ROBBERS OF TIME ARE THE PAST AND FUTURE

It is said that the present is a gift. Do we appreciate it, or give it away? When we live too much in the past, which is history, we have old skins clinging to us. The future is not yet born, and rather than allowing that to seem like some fated scenario, we can choose to be creators with it by being fully alive in the gift of the now. When the past, like a muffled, disguised traveller, lurks in both present and future scenarios, it is not so easy to tap into the ongoing timings available to us with their fresh air messages. Not just smog but misalignments occur and we cast blame on externals too readily.

The art of timing isn't that demanding really. It is often about being prepared to change some habits. If something isn't serving us, why not change it? I am sure that our inner timekeepers, who love the musical harmonies of the little cosmos within us, are not too happy when (again to quote Einstein), we allow a kind of insanity by *"doing the same things over and over again, and expecting different results".*

OUR MIRROR THE MOON

So as to avoid the annoying tendency of getting stuck in a rut let's have a look at some basic ways to be in tune with the Moon, one of the most important time keepers we have available. We get our word lunacy from Luna, the Roman name for Moon! For example, the Moon is Lundi in French, De lun in Cornish, dies Lunae in Latin and Luna in Romanian.

The Moon, in its phases of beginning, fullness, decline, followed by the promise of renewal, rules timing at a deep level. Way back in time our ancestors viewed the Moon as the giver of birth and watched its cycles, from new to full to dark to new phase again, with great awe.

The phases during the month can be easily obtained from a diary, the web or an astronomical ephemeris. Getting yourself a Moon diary or almanac with the lunation cycles and following the waxing, waning phases may be a nice edition to your life. Navigating your responses and even choosing phases for events could be timely!

With the research born of time we also can view it with awe. Here are some reasons why it is can be useful to feel in alignment with the Moon.

We know the Moon rules the tides and is intrinsically bonded with the Earth. Its phases, waxing and waning, affect us in many ways. They are the angles of union, flow, separation and reunion with the Sun. They are also the natural rhythms we all have between our inner and outer worlds.

We know of the once a month Full Moon being blamed for the rise in crime, emotional outbursts and mental instability. In our own lives we witness overflows of emotional energies and tensions, unexpected occurrences and a feeling of overload. I have talked with many hospital staff who confirm that Full Moon dates are busier and more critical. Primary and special needs teachers are fully aware of this monthly occurrence.

The Full Moon date being well documented is worthy of note. In a positive way we can choose that time to bring things to completion and public attention, especially in business projects or for celebrations.

Our bodies are made up of over 87% fluid and our own tides sway us in their dance of change and need for periodic involvement and retreat from activity. How often do we comply with these? The Moon's dance is a beautifully simple cycle in the month that we can observe and feel part of if we choose.

AWARENESS

Because we have many ingrained patterns, we can often reach a crisis when something has to give and change. Our bodies play up or the house, office or our technological equipment cause problems which often mirror that we have overload, a clogged mind and the like. If you don't believe that, check out how you have been feeling leading up to overflows in the house, circuits blowing, appliances breaking down. Ironically, when one thing happens, others often do. An opportunity to reassess not just the things that need fixing but our inner balance and emotions beckons.

The Sun and Moon, the two eyes of heaven according to the Egyptians in times past, are in opposition at a Full Moon and there is a pull on our polar ways of looking at things. Take for example the case at the time of writing this when the Moon is in the sign of Taurus with the Sun in the month of Scorpio - its opposite sign. The need to be still and to enjoy the senses of nature, the body and the arts, along with the awareness of the need for release and breakdown of established ways hold sway.

It is easy to check each month which zodiac sign the Full Moon is in; try being a fledgling astrologer. Simple though the words below are they are useful to apply to your life whatever Sun sign you are.

In *Aries*: Be aware of impulsiveness but be ready for action and new starts if you want them.
In *Taurus*: Nurture what you have and enjoy your pleasures and nature's gifts, but watch overindulgence.
In *Gemini*: Gather your ideas together and share them. A good date for exchanging knowledge and facts.
In *Cancer*: It's easy now to feel extra subjective and need time to yourself. Don't hide but honour your rhythms.
In *Leo*: You want to be part of the party and loved. Use the date for enjoying culture and romance.

In *Virgo*: Don't overdo excess and do take time to mentor yourself and help others and self in small ways.
In *Libra*: Get relationships into perspective and reach out to others. Don't overextend and get worn out though.
In *Scorpio*: Be conscious of deeper feelings and unresolved issues. Transform them and be kind.
In *Sagittarius:* Have some adventure and feel grateful for the path you are on. Don't be too direct.
In *Capricorn*: A date to be industrious and honour your own authority in a calm way. Don't let pride rule you.
In *Aquarius*: A friendly day, so use it to think bigger and out of the box. Be a team player.
In *Pisces*: Indulge your imagination and be creative. Don't play victim.

These were just a few keywords to help avoid being over the top with reactions on the Full Moon.

A research project done by British Telecom some years ago now resulted in conclusions that mobile phone usage was much higher around the Full Moon time. Maybe this is because of heightened feelings and need for communication as pressure builds. And it does build. It is tangible, and we see things which have been pending come to fruition. The electrical potential of the body is greater and fluid levels are too. The 'bloating' factor comes into its own then! Haemorrhaging during or after surgical operations is higher. Weight loss groups have told me that people weigh slightly more at the Full Moon than they would otherwise.

In the redwood forests in the United States trees are marked with the symbols of the New Moon and Full Moon so that their value is shown accordingly. The reason? As fluids are higher at the Full Moon, the sap can weaken the wood's quality.

Sap also engorges trees more during the waxing moon and can also attract the death watch beetle in forests, which then devastates the harvest. Contracts for cutting of these trees often call for cutting during the waning phase, after the Full Moon has passed.

Many years ago I had a hobby making jewellery from silver. I quickly found that at the time of the Full Moon the soldering of silver became more problematical. My instructor wryly commented that it was a common occurrence when working with silver and had learnt to take that for granted!

Traditionally, silver is associated with the Moon. Our ancestors definitely knew a great deal.

From the word *Moon* we get our words month and menstruation. Women who share a living space find their menstrual cycles start to synchronise – an example of our connectedness at an energy level. The importance of the Moon in timing is therefore paramount for our own and nature's rhythms.

If you are born around a Full Moon and indeed the New Moon time of the month, expect to feel extra sensitive. A memory gets kindled from when we were born, for that pattern is within us and our emotions heighten.

Mainly seen as feminine throughout cultures, because of her dance with the Sun god, although there are cases of the other way around, the interplay between the Moon and the Sun and Earth fascinated us. Without the Sun, life would die here on Earth; that is one side of the picture though for, *'where the Sun always shines there is a desert below'*.

The night light and daylight are both equally necessary for life. In certain myths from different cultures we are warned that to look directly on the face of the sun god bodes crisis. We would not be able to handle the glare of full consciousness and would be burnt up in its power! The Sun psychologically represents our essence; the discovery of our shining potential.

We know just how hard it is to be truly ourselves and to let light into our crevices. To see ourselves as a whole can be just too real. So we create habits and masks to feel safe, to unwrap a bit at a time, to unfold with our seasons. This is where our Moon sign reigns.
Pleasing others to fit into life can ultimately make us question how authentic we are being. But until we choose to not be a 'photocopy' and instead claim our authenticity, our real self, we slot into roles very easily which seem to serve us until we reach a cul-de-sac, have a wakeup call and perhaps then make new choices.

From childhood, we start to see ourselves through the phase and sign the Moon was in when we were born, allowing for the fluctuation of mood and shades of light and dark. This mirror can be likened to our self- image, how we *see* ourselves and thus often limit ourselves. Our inner Moon represents our need to belong, to feel safe and nurture what we are bonded to. As we grow, not just chronologically, but hopefully in wisdom we can enrich how we work and relate to beginnings and change.

In the lunar month phases of 29.5 days, we experience the total cycle of New (seeding) Moon, waxing crescent Moon, Full (half of the circle) and then the waning Moon phase until the three days before the New Moon again. Those three days are called the magical dark

Moon. A potent reprieve period for really allowing timing to be our friend in ways not immediately obvious! If you check when there is a New Moon in the month then it is easy to see the dates of the three days before and plan to use them wisely.

Whether this is winding something down, retreating, meditating, or allowing the inner world to be a bit more chaotic, the well has to empty and await the seeding of the New Moon time. I usually try to take at least some time in that patch for going to ground. Our tribal ancestors would have seen that as essential to the flow and health of the community.

SEIZING THE MOMENT

In times past, that moment of the New Moon was used for rites, ceremonies, and making wishes. Do you ever do that, even in a simple manner?

If it worked for those communities, and it must have done as they continued doing it...., be very present with yourself at that special moment and ***intend*** what you want for the coming lunar month. Intention is valuable, setting the stage for time's passage and our journey in it. It empowers us.

It can be compared to an archer eyeing the target board, and then letting the arrow go. Once it has flown, it does its own thing doesn't it? The same can apply to setting an intent at a New Moon date and then getting on with life. The rest follows. Like any technique, it improves with practice.

Sometimes, **simplicity** is the most powerful gift we can be given and utilize. We sometimes feel we need to try hard and that things have to be a bit difficult to be worthy! Even if we don't consciously think this it can still run us. We distrust 'ease'. Have you considered the two syllables, dis-ease?

Naturally we need to know what we are doing, to have trained at a subject maybe, and of course be responsible with our actions. However, when we clear the debris of over complication and angst, as well as knowing our physical limits when it comes to saying yes or no to people and taking on too much, everything magically falls into place.

It doesn't just aid us but also others who benefit from that ease and don't have to deal with our rushing, our stress and even anger. This is when timing is happiest!

When did you last choose to relate to life that way and how did it make you feel?

Some of us seem to be born with that gift and some of us are fortunate to been encouraged that way by wise teachers and family. Yet, for those of us who do complicate things and take on too much just 'because it is there', we can either get wake up calls from life and learn from how other people react to us, or just be kinder on ourselves.

With the spirit of timing we are encouraged to trust how we move through our day and tasks so there is a healthy relationship between our actions, our timing and awareness of what we are doing from moment to moment. Being a creator with those hours and choices in a day, recognising limits, recognising the power of remembering to breathe consciously and doing things with grace, brings dividends.

Think about the timing of breathing! We have to breathe out (let go), as much as breathe in (hold). They are of equal importance, so why not apply that rhythm to other things?

If we didn't take our first breath of the Earth's atmosphere nothing would ever start for us. Cycles are set into motion then within us and are mirrored in the heavens. Techniques such as rebirthing, regression, and meditation bring us back in touch with our cycles when we feel at odds with life. Retracing our lives to see the bigger picture and thus clarifying our *daily way of handling things* is a good exercise. We can easily be our own worst enemy and sabotage what is good for us. And let's not forget the gift of humour!

On the note of humour, have you noticed how naturally humorous people, not necessarily the joke makers, have a great sense of timing? There is a relaxed air and the capacity to pause at the right time. Indeed, when we are most relaxed and not taking ourselves too seriously, our own humour shines through, our faces relax and taking a bit of time out doesn't matter so much.

Going back to the planets, the word planet (planete) comes from the word wanderer. Whenever there are strong configurations between them, and not just with the lunar angles, we here on terra firma feel the impact.

There have been challenging angles in 2016 between the slower moving planets, Uranus, Pluto and Neptune and Saturn.

In myth, Saturn and Uranus were father and son, neither wanting to be superseded by the other.

FATHER TIME

Saturn's Greek name was Chronos, from which we have inherited our words, chronic and chronological.

Father Time likes to take his time and, in its 29-and-a-half-year cycle around the Sun, Saturn highlights times in our lives, roughly every seven years, when maturation occurs and ideally new life cycles. If we are fortunate, we see at least three Saturn returns in our lifetime.

Uranus, known in Holst's planets suite as the magician, has an 84-year cycle, staying in each of the 12 signs of the zodiac seven years. These two planets have been mirroring the pull between old, established ways, Saturn, and wake up calls from the trickster, Uranus. With research, it has been found that Uranus is linked in a tense aspect to the epicentre of an earthquake when one occurs.
I have seen over many years how transits of Uranus to our birth charts can signal breakthroughs, eureka (light bulb) moments and sudden changes of orientation. Also, when too many cracks have been papered over to avoid change and growth, or overload of stress, nervous breakdowns can occur. Research never appealed to me much until I delved into astrology!

When Uranus was discovered in 1781, there was the shift here in Britain from an agricultural based society to an industrial one. Rebellions such as the French Revolution were building up. And the USA as we know it today was founded. All change! This is interesting material as, when a planet is discovered, it correlates with events here on Earth linked with the mythological meaning of that body. In this case, Uranus, the lightning god, inventive maverick and bringer of sweeping change and reform.

Neptune, the god of the oceans, has a 164 year cycle. At present, it is unlikely we will live that long! Its movement relating to its position when we were born can highlight in the 14 year cycles it spends roughly in each zodiac sign, times of shifting beliefs and soul and creative growth.

If you are good at your multiplication tables check out the seven and fourteen year cycles in your life.

There are many, many more cycles, but this book is designed to look at some general ones and provide an idea and glimpse of what we are all part of. There are very precise astronomical/astrological ones, which need to be calculated for each individual and I have so enjoyed exploring them with clients over the decades.

But do have a think about other cycles of time which you tend to follow.... Are there numbers and days of the week or times of the year which you really resonate with? Are they serving you well? If so, do you consciously use them to bring about good things?

THE POWER OF SEVEN

The seven year cycle has been well documented. It is said the body with its cells renews itself every seven years, so why not other layers of our being? Nature, such a revealing mirror, visibly as well as invisibly, sheds skins and metamorphoses. We do the same but, apart from the obvious ageing process, it is less visible. Without the inner cooperation that nature has we can choose, with our free will, to ignore our own inner promptings and get pot bound in our minds. And we wonder why things keep repeating or get stagnant!

There is a famous picture of the god Saturn by the artist Goya, gobbling up his children. Saturn did this, in case you are wondering why, to prevent them taking over his role as king of the gods and men. His father Uranus tried to get rid of him as well; it is strange how generations don't learn!

Remembering that as Saturn is father time we are being shown how we gobble up time and yet don't always accept the passing of it and the ageing process. We can't hold back the tide, as King Canute back in ancient Britain tried to do as he sat on a throne on a beach and commanded the waves to retreat! A funny analogy, but we often do the same with our lives, don't we?

One of his sons, Jupiter, escaped this fate with the help of his mother. He grew to be a larger than life god, full of adventure, optimism and the thirst to learn. He is of course our largest planet, spending 12 years in each zodiac sign. Every 12 years it enters our own sun sign which is easily checked out, and we can choose to expand our boundaries and have more confidence.

On a yearly scale, be aware of the month when the Sun, your vitality, is in the opposite zodiac sign to the month when you were born. This is a time when the tidal rhythms are at an ebb and energy can feel lower. The month before your birthday is another time period when the life force is quieter, and, like the three days of the dark Moon preceding the New Moon once a month, an ideal time to have more rest, a relaxed holiday and reflection.
Not to worry you, but it is remarkable how many people die in the month before their birthday, or the hour before dawn. Not all of course! Our bodies are part of nature's cycles and know the right time.

Simple though some of these examples are of natural timing in our lives they are also powerful, as simple things so often are.

Our friendly inner timekeepers struggle to match and have their say in our busy world. Just recognise them!

NOTES FOR YOURSELF

Chapter Three

MAGICAL COSMIC CYCLES AND NUMBERS

"The world is full of magic things, patiently waiting for our senses to grow sharper"

W.B Yeats

Maybe, like myself, you found as a child that you were drawn to certain numbers in particular? Or you found that certain ones come into your orb on regular occasions as in house numbers, car registrations, in birth dates of people you are close to and so on?
Is this coincidence, or some kind of magnetism at work?
Maybe you haven't looked too closely at this, but like other ideas mentioned in the previous two chapters, it might be fun to take a window of time out to see if this holds true for you.
As we noticed earlier numbers play quite a big part in astronomy and planetary cycles. The seven year cycles seem to show a regular cycle of endings, pruning and shedding!
The 11 year peak sun spot cycle which plays a large part in migration activity, wars, uprisings, shows a peak of 'mass excitement', as scientists have noticed, around that time, and a lowered incidence (trough) half way through the 11 years.

Dr Tokata, back in the last century, discovered that the 'flocculation index' of human blood serum was affected by the onset of the sunspot cycle peak. It is generally accepted that peak sunspot activity does stimulate higher levels of activity in the mineral, vegetable, animal and human kingdoms. We can easily find out when this phenomenon happens and hopefully keep an eye on our behaviour accordingly!

Cycles are important, whether they be economic, natural ones, crops, wars, epidemic; the list goes on. Foundations for the study of cycles exist and are there to learn from. There are cycles as diverse as the soy bean cycle to cotton cycles to women's skirts lengths, to the 'biggies' such as the planets, a few cycles of which we have looked at.

I find something rather soothing in knowing this. Whether some of those cycles touch our personal lives or not, there appears to be rhyme and reason to why they exist and are observed and monitored by the scientific world.

So, as with numbers, are there cycles that seem to repeat in your life? They say that what goes around comes around, and when a pattern repeats in our lives, maybe a similar set of circumstances to a previous one, we are being shown something to be aware of.

I think sometimes it is more important that, rather than getting caught up with the research in all this, that just being cognisant and at times in awe of the intelligence in the universe, sensing the beauty of the workings of life, we can really belong in a vibrant way on this planet. Mystery, and knowing there is something bigger, far bigger, than the fragments we experience, lifts us out of the *"commonplace and into the rare"*. But back to numbers in our lives. Numbers are symbolic.

Sym-bolism, that which brings things together, combines reason and higher meaning. In times past, mathematicians and the like were seen as holy and divine.
Numbers held meanings and secrets, as well as being useful tools. Children get fascinated by them, and, if we are lucky to have enthusiasm and imagination instilled into the teaching of them, they can take us to interesting places in our minds.
The significance of numbers shows up in the make up of plants, flowers, sacred buildings and our own bodies.

I thought I would highlight some of these perfect designs so we can perhaps look at how parts of us at least can emulate and use that knowledge. If it works for nature and beautiful architecture it can work for us!

Let's explore.

BEING IN PROPORTION

Beauty is always present in higher mathematics. Maybe we can view beauty as a science unto itself? Certainly, the proportions in crystalline structures, geometrical shapes such as the pentagon,

hexahedron, tetrahedron, octahedron, dodecahedron shapes are beautifully depicted in nature's offspring of snowflakes, plants and crystals.
Let's see why unconsciously we are drawn to certain numbers...

Stand with your legs astride, arms out to the side and head erect and you have the shape of man as the pentagram, fivefold.
We carry the five-ness of life around with us. Linked with the hexagonal shape, their fusion has the same shape and proportions as the nucleic connections of the DNA molecule which carries the genetic code. Two pairs of these joined by a golden mean rectangle (more on that) rise in a three dimensional spiral.

In numerology, five was called the number of free will and creativity; sometimes it was referred to as 'evil' by some minds and schools of thought, as free will is open to being abused. It was also linked with healers and doctors who in studies used to comment on the regular occurrence of health crises and breakthroughs at the fifth hour, day, week or even month and year.
Indeed, in any on-going situation one can observe on the fifth hour, day or week and so forth, there is some change of energy or mode of communication. Four, the preceding number, is squareness, safety and routine and five breaks the mould in some way. A strange

thought? Well do try it out. I have observed that pattern at work on many occasions.
I am aware this is stretching logic a bit, or is it? It involves thinking outside the box but, once again, the things and phenomena we let glide by or through us without making connections are getting an airing here and wish to be read.

NUMBERS IN NATURE

Five-ness is linked with the creative, living principle, sexuality and freedom. Philosophers of old made that point often in their writings. Angles between planets of 72 and 144 degrees in a birth chart, based on the core coordinates of date, time and longitude and latitude, highlight one's attunement to those things. 72 degrees is a quintile - a *fifth* of the circle.
Five is dominant in the substructure of all living things. The rose family is one of those based on five, as are all the flowers of the edible, fruit bearing plants. The centre of an apple when cut open displays the five-ness of the pentagram

The six-fold and eightfold numbers are most characteristic of the geometry of mineral structures and their beauty.

Tulips, lilies and poppies are six-fold in their properties. Snowflakes are hexagonal, six-fold, in appearance and the shape of insulin is six fold also in its structure. The number seven shows up in petalled plants such as nightshade, belladonna and tomatoes. The very exotic flowers, called the flowers of love, such as the orchid, passion flower and again the rose, are all ruled by pentagonal (five) symmetry.

Remember the outstretched shape of our body which looks like a pentacle with five appendages – arms, legs, and head?

The Fibonacci series with its golden section, Phi, golden ratio or rectangle 'secret', is a mathematical measurement found throughout nature, the proportions of the human body and sacred architecture. It is well worth reading up about if you are not familiar as, once again, the timing, spacing and beauty in numbers, become apparent all around us. And for those who know about it, let's remember to admire its perfect place in life. What intelligence wove this design so it appeared with such constancy?

Maybe, as I mentioned earlier, that as the physicist James Jeans said, scientists are beginning to sense that the ***universe is indeed becoming more and more like a great mind and not a great machine.***

Phi, or the golden ratio, is the name given to a mathematical proportion that was originally measured out with rope! As early as the building of the Parthenon and the pyramids it was used to give them their harmonious shapes. Instinctively, it was used by architects, artists and the like, and in the 12th century an Italian mathematician, Fibonacci, originally named Leonardo of Pisa, discovered the properties of the numerical series. Thus the name Fibonacci has come down to us today.

THE MATHEMATICS OF BEAUTY

In the context of this book, very simply, here are a few lines about it. The Fibonacci series is linked with the fact that the ratio of one number to the next is 1: 1.618... called phi or the Golden Mean. **0+1=1 +1=2+1=3 +2=5 +3=8 +5=13, etc.** These number proportions of 1, 2, 3, 5, 8, 13, 21, 34, 55, 89, 144 and on into infinity is a sequence where each number is the sum of the previous two and run through proportions, animate and inanimate. They resonate with the golden mean ratio, phi, 1: 0.6180. Even the naval in our bodies, once we have passed early childhood, sits at that ratio proportion in our frame.

Examples of that proportion show up beautifully in the mollusc and nautilus shell spirals, our DNA, and in antlers. It is also found in the cochlea of the inner ear and the proportions between nail, finger, hand width, forearm and upper arm.
It is super-imposable on the foetus of man and animal and exists in the growth patterns of many plants. It shows up in the distribution of the sunflower's seeds and the fact that the Fibonacci number of 55 shows up in clockwise spirals which are then overlaid onto either 34 or 89 (two other Fibonacci numbers) counter clockwise spirals. The seed distribution of a cactus also has the proportion, and as mentioned earlier, so do flowers having five petals or multiples of five.

If you look at a central stem of a plant you will see the Fibonacci series at work and play: three leaves in five turns, five leaves in eight turns. They are also found in the ratio of male to female bees in honey bee hives and in the breeding patterns of rabbits!

In the branching of plants and trees in their natural state the numbers are always present. In the heavens, the spiralling galaxies behave in the same way. ***As above, so below.***

PLEASING FORMS

Wherever there is an intensification of beauty and harmony of form, the golden mean proportion will be present. And our ancestors copied this in art and sculpture: Da Vinci, Seurat, Durat, as examples. Michelangelo's *David* is a prime example of this.
In sacred architecture a bridge gets created between the cosmos, nature and man/woman. The Parthenon, the pyramids, gothic cathedral windows, especially the rose design in the latter, contain these proportions.

In recent times, the Eden project's educational centre called The Core, in Cornwall, has been designed using Fibonacci numbers and plant spirals proportions. Peter Randall-Paige's design sculpture called *The Seed* at the centre of The Core is apparently based on the spirals found in seeds and sunflowers and pine cones. So, time doesn't wither the message of the beauty of mathematics and nature's favourite shape and formula!

Living in or visiting structures containing this golden ratio gives such a feeling of wellbeing. Needless to say, our modern buildings, homes and offices, with their 90 degree corners and box like shapes, create tension without our always knowing it. To walk from the architecture which contains open angles, and better still the Fibonacci proportions, into the 'boxes' we mainly live and breathe in, wakes us up to the difference. Even with breathing, the rate and rhythm changes from ease to tautness. Nature doesn't lean towards ninety degree angles.

Rectangles where the ratio of the length of the short side to the long side is 0.618, was noted by Greek architects as the most visually pleasing, and its designs were used to construct important buildings in previous times.

Incidentally, the credit cards we carry on us are in the proportion of the golden mean! Maybe that is one reason it is so easy to use them! What else can you think of containing that proportion?

Modern designers are becoming aware of the benefits of using this proportion in their work to please the eye and all that follows from that!

The expression, 'Time is Money’, has something to answer to when it comes to cutting corners and not valuing quality as much as we could.

THE MIRROR OF NATURE

I wanted to include the magical phi number and its series of Fibonacci numbers in this chapter. I feel it is an important part of the art of understanding of timing and cycles so as to embrace numbers, not just as abstract maths, but for their intrinsic role in the make up of this planet and all that occupies it!
There is a relationship that can be proven with numbers, giving rise to a series of shapes that show up in nature. These can be translated by creative minds into forms which we love to look at and which stand the course of time. Maybe it is not too far fetched to say they have a healing effect on us?

So, why are these numbers important, almost magical in our world? The 'divine' proportion contains remarkable properties - harmony, balance and regeneration. *Harmony* in the designs in nature, below and above us, *balance* as in the spiral in the inner ear and *regeneration* as a force in the shapes and solids that form the basis of life from the DNA to the movements and contour of the universe.

Surely, if we live not just in an ecologically friendly way with the natural world but in awareness and harmony with its shapes and proportions, we will resonate with our own inner navigation of

timing of growth, knowing when to catch the wave and when to drop anchor!
The good news is we don't have to be mathematicians to explore this. We are surrounded by the proportion. How often do you walk into a building and for no obvious reason feel very comfortable? The place may be quite sparse, poorly furnished and simple even, but our body and soul feel freer. There may well be elements of the divine proportion there mathematically. We soak it up and don't question why. We just know how we feel.

As an aid for being in rhythm and time with our lives it can help to have those shapes, spirals and art work around us. Obtain a photo or picture or sculpture model of something beautiful containing this proportion. Sunflowers, nautilus shells, sacred architecture are some, but there are many others.

It is no surprise really when we visit art galleries such as The National Portrait Gallery in London and Uffizi in Florence and gaze on the work of the Old Masters, that we are drawn in and feel more whole and inspired. We are not really looking for the mathematical proportions but they are there all the same. Knowing that our bodies are made of those numbers and proportions, that our basic DNA is of it, can be comforting in a world where artificial lines, harsh angles and the like are everywhere.

Becoming more conscious of these gives us freedom to breathe more easily, physically and emotionally.
Naturally, our sense of being in time is enhanced.

MUSIC AND OUR INNER TIMING

In Music these numbers, resonances and ratios are also present. Whole books are worthy of that subject and I recommend you finding them.
To make it applicable to our subject here about getting the best out of timing and our cycles though, let us look at some ideas.

I talked about the ratios, we can also call them harmonics, in nature, the body and architecture. In music composition whole number ratios of musical harmonics, the octave, 3rds, 4ths, 5ths, correspond to an underlying numerical framework which exists in chemistry, atomic physics, crystals, architecture and botany. The relationships in the periodic table of elements, from which all matter is formed, resemble the overtone structure in music.

The structure of the atom itself contains ratios which resemble the harmonic principle of music. The scientist, naturalist and writer J. Goethe wrote that Music is liquid architecture; architecture is frozen music. This is more than just a pretty phrase. Frank Lloyd Wright, the amazing American architect, with buildings in the likes of Chicago and New York, apparently saw aspects of his work in that quote.

Old writings show that in the past the Chinese thought that a piece of music was an energy formula!

It is no coincidence that we are drawn to, even find healing in, certain composers.

3:4 time, for example, may feel 'at home' for you. So play it!

BACH THE ALCHEMIST

In relation to the golden mean, did you know that J.S Bach's music incorporated intervals into his music that bore the same relationship to each other as the as numbers in the Fibonacci series, creating the same golden mean proportions that we saw earlier in examples?

Just as sacred architecture, ancient and modern, display a visual harmony, so music displays a vibratory harmony. In music therapy

Bach's music has been used to help manic depression, or what is now referred to as bi-polar conditions. With the beauty of the Fibonacci series we can move back into better rhythms.
We don't need to have illnesses to gain benefit from time to time with his music when we feel out of balance. Bach is not everyone's cup of tea, but therapeutically his music formulas are sheer genius and beneficial.

TIME CYCLES

Time cycles in business and the stock market prove an interesting way of following the Fibonacci series of numbers. They have been, and still are, much utilised and examined. The Kondratieff Cycle, a common, often quoted cycle of financial and economic behaviour, of 55 years, was given its name from a Russian economist in the 1920's.

The 54/55 year cycle was recognised by the Mayans, who knew a thing or two about calendars and cycles! 55 is a Fibonacci number and ratios of it link with market movements and, as we have seen, the distribution of seeds and spirals in plants.
It is not choosy where it makes its mark – from nature to economics.

THE POWER OF THE CIRCLE AND 360 DEGREES

In the circle of the astronomical year, we have the months and numbers therein. Twelve into 360 is 30 and it is fascinating to observe and indeed work with timing and observing events personally and globally in that framework.

The 1930's Wall Street Trader W D Gann made good money out of working with the astronomical cycles pertaining to segments of 30 degrees. He used fractions of the circle: 1/4, 1/3, 1/8 etc. to count the number of days, weeks, months between highs and lows.

In the context of this book, I will only be referring to a way of working with our own business or personal happenings in a simple but revealing way. However, Gann certainly knew and worked the stock market by using the cycles and daily movements of the planets in general with remarkable success. His work was more concerned with those cycles and not the star signs of popular usage as we know them in the media.

Astro-economists work by matching financial data to planetary cycles. They feed in sets of prices, commodities, and exchange rates and look for a MATCH with a planetary cycle. A whole field of study unto itself.

For the purpose here of exploring how to turn challenges into opportunities, I want to touch on how we can be observant of the times when things change and reach crossroads.

Whether you want to look back at the sequence of a certain event and its outcome, an ongoing one, or a new one which has just started, choose it and be detective...

An event of significance happens and, in the count of 15, 30, 45, 60, 90, 135, 150, 180, 270, 315, 330, 360, just watch how it undergoes changes.
Maybe it is 30 or 45 hours, days, weeks, months, sometimes years, but at those points something happens, especially if there are unanswered questions surrounding it, and the outcome is pending.

Particularly at tense points on this grid such as 45, 90 and 180, we can expect a change of some kind, sometimes a crisis or something being revealed. These numbers are angles of the 360 degree circle which astrologers also use to check the flows and tensions between planets and behaviour on Earth.
I tracked some events in recent history as well as in my own life, and time and again saw a pattern emerging. You might like to track something in yours?

When we look at what was happening in the elections in the USA in November 2016, we see there is an opposition of 180 degrees from Pluto to the nation's Sun in Cancer when the Founding Fathers set up the constitution on July 4th 1776.

A BIG CYCLE ON

The zodiac sign of Cancer represents, along with other characteristics, our innate security needs, what has been nurtured and established and even created a protective shell around. Pluto's function in world affairs and in a country's birth chart (yes, countries have their chart just as we do) is to be rather volcanic and bring out the shadow side and primal undercurrents.

About 248 years ago (its length of orbit) Pluto was in opposition to the nation's Sun sign of Cancer then, and now, one big cycle on, we are seeing unprecedented change in the established ways of doing things in government.

It will gradually move on and away from that opposition degree but it takes time to re adjust, especially with such a slow moving body like Pluto. Mythologically, Pluto, god of Hades, the underworld, very much did things his way, representing the death of the old. In our own birth charts it shows up areas of life ready for transformation, dealing with power plays and shows ways to learn, sometimes from pain. We get our words plutocratic and plutonium from Pluto. Wake up calls and political volcanic eruption are not uncommon when Pluto 'comes to call'.

With an opposition, (as we saw earlier, the full moon every month shows this on a small scale amplifying how we are feeling), a major transit like this definitely awakens lurking issues and is unstable to the establishment and outmoded ways of governing. Oppositions of 180 degrees to an initial date will always give perspective and sometimes swing the other way. Uncomfortable maybe and challenging certainly, but polarising happens when things have got stagnant. 180 degrees is the half way mark on the cosmic clock and circle, a trough and a pulling away from what was 'set up'.

TIME CHANGES

So, if we apply this to our own lives, we could take a happening like starting a new job, a meeting of importance, a new relationship or change of location, and track its progress. Whether in minor or major ways, we can look out for the currents of change at the 30 hours, days, weeks, months, years junctions. A bit like crossroads where we have to take stock. So mark the dates when you initiate something and observe and be prepared for the changes. Change is the one constant in life, whether we like it or not.

2016 was indeed the year of a big need for a change from old systems, thus we see unpredictable results and happenings in politics and indeed our personal lives. 'Nine' is the end of a cycle and 2016 added up to a nine. 2=0=1=6= nine. Something has to give and to move on to a new level. A relinquishing of control in some way is at work.

Look at your own life and check out the numbers. We feel like tying up loose ends, releasing burdens and outmoded structure and attachments. 2017 is a 'One' year; new starts and new attitudes. What do we plan and put fresh air into now?

The numbers 1-9 see a progression of values as guides to growth. Numerology books and courses abound, and just for the purpose here of linking them with timing, again have a think of what numbers draw you.

One represents the independent person or start of an enterprise. A day for initiating by self.

Two represents partnership and duality, cooperation. A day for relationship and sharing a project.

Three represents the triad, perspective, sociability and expansion. A day to share creativity with others.

Four represents organisation, stability and form. A day for details, admin, routine, taking stock.

Five represents change, freedom, innovation. A day for shifting and allowing change for things to grow.

Six represents adjustment, harmony and beauty. A day for domesticity and family and the arts.

Seven represents the thinker, philosophy and inner quest. A day for alone time, intuition and study.

Eight represents mastery of the material world and business. The octave takes the key note in music to a higher level and can enrich self-expression in work and goals. A day for progress with finance, goals and reputation.

Nine represents humanitarian expression and some sacrifice of old ways. The inner spirit has a big say. A day for tying up loose ends, helping others, not overdoing things.

Ten represents One 1+0=1. A day to review, and start something which can last for a while.

Eleven is sometimes seen as a master number and represents power and inspiration to be used wisely. When we hand our power over to others we disempower ourselves and reduce the 'eleven' to a 'two' digit, with the emphasis more on the partner or 'other' in our life. If your full birth date, month and full year digits add up to an eleven, try to avoid serving others too much and overlooking your own personal greatness and talent.

Numbers and their meaning have come down to us from many sources and we get our geometrical shapes from them of course: The triangle, *three*, the cube, *four*, the pentagon, *five*, the hexagon, *six* and so forth. Plato termed them the platonic solids.

When working with your timing, try using the date of the month - reduce double numbers to one number - for specific events and how you want ideally to spend your day. Maybe explore them more. You can also apply them to the current year as we saw by adding the digits together and reducing to one digit.

In this chapter I have endeavoured to pull together ideas, some simple and some more complex, to again explore the bigger web we are part of. These ideas and systems of thought which I have looked at over the years have intrigued me. I hope you also find them of value and addition to your life.

At the end of the day, all this knowledge is out there and within us. Understanding the magical framework of time, so we can use it to make life a bit easier for ourselves, brings into play the resonances, numbers, harmonics around us, which we all are made of and part of.

From the very small ratios in the atom to the large cosmic cycles above us we are forever linked.

They are magical numbers and cycles indeed. Our birth right and wise navigator.

NOTES FOR YOURSELF

Chapter Four

IN–TUITION AND TRUSTING YOUR INNER COMPASS

"Bright star were I as steadfast as thou art"

Keats

In the last chapter we got into a lot of numbers and some maths. This one is different.

I was never a lover of maths, and it is nothing far short of a miracle that for the first fifteen years of working as an astrologer before there were computers, or at least the programmes for astrology, I was doing all the calculations, logarithms and the like by hand.

How did I do it when I was unable to learn from the teachers I had at school anything abstract and complicated with maths, algebra, geometry and the like? Well.... It was my passion for the subject. Knowing I had no choice but to master the left brain side of astronomy and the star maps if I wanted to be an explorer of what is above and how it related to life on Earth, I persevered.

When in time I had computer programmes to calculate the positions of the planets, there was a little bit of me that missed the craft of taking time to see the chart of a person come to life under my fingers.

In that process of drawing the symbols and aspects, I could get a feeling of the stories and heritage from the person's family line, the flows and blockages in the diagram which was coming alive for me as I calculated and drew it.

A TOOLBOX TO USE THROUGH LIFE'S CHANGES

When sitting and talking with the client, discussing their life and time passages, a journey develops. Plus an endorsement of what they know at heart and which is timely to hear from a different source as well. There is also information which is timely to look at and explore. I let the energy of the chart and its timings guide me. I have been asked many times if I believe in it, and I can honestly answer that it's not a matter of belief but a knowingness.
I know it works as a map of the psyche and cycles of our lives and it is a great toolbox with which to explore meaning, purpose and timing of change. I have never been bored with the subject.

Looking back over a long life I realise just how much curiosity, intuition and inner freedom were my friends. Intuition guided me more than I knew consciously. Has it you? Or do you follow rote and planning to the letter? Or a bit of both? Have a check and weigh it up. How youthful do *you* feel when healthy curiosity is your friend?

As a youngster I loved maps and the outdoors; I was better finding my way in the countryside or wilds than the city. That hasn't changed much in my life! Maps - the paper variety - can be faulty but so can a sat nav and the like. Cul-de sacs, ending up in a field, being directed miles off course, can be the by product of the latter occasionally.

With our inner mapping are we also at times out of touch with it now due to outer signals distracting and bombarding them. Too many signposts, signal lights, and traffic clutter our inner landscape.

MYTHS WHICH ARE RELEVANT TODAY

I thought we might have a look at some myths and stories and pay them a visit.

We could try the route suggested by Peter Pan when he said to Wendy, *"....second star to the right and straight on till morning",* but that was the direction to Neverland! Even birds might find it hard to follow those directions, no matter how good their navigation skills. But imagination and the heart do take us places the reason cannot, and that quote has come down to us as one of the most loved, along with... *"Do you believe in fairies?"* And, *"To die will be an awfully big adventure."* It all takes a bucketful of something called faith! Our inner world can feel rather like going into Alice's Wonderland; nothing is quite as it seems there. *"Curiouser and curiouser,"* as Alice said. Our inner geography, being unknown territory compared to how we live and see our outer world and experiences, is populated with stories, useful or otherwise. We get glimpses in dreams and intuitions.

Ask yourself or a friend what their inner landscape, or terrain is looking and feeling like at this stage in life. It may stretch imagination somewhat but it doesn't take long to start seeing, like a picture in a frame, the geographical landmarks. For example, is it looking barren, colourful, mountainous. Does it have changeable weather, smooth or calm seas?

Is it a surreal, or a classic landscape? Is it populated or solitary?

I find that after exploring this with my clients, and we continue to clear some debris of stuff that is not working, the picture starts changing. For everyday purposes, try beaming sunlight at the landscape if it looks a bit sad, gloomy or stormy and, when the sunlight passes on, the scene often changes offering new possibilities.

These things need to be experienced to feel like potential tools for change.

How often do we use the terms 'monsters', 'ogre', angel', 'trickster', to describe a strong situation or larger than life person? They are

built into our vocabulary from the myths, scriptures and the stories which have come through to us from our families and culture.
Our ancestors wove stories and character profiles initially from the stars and planets, and a myth was seen as a sacred story set in a time and place outside history. The stories also described transition points in history, for example the shift from the matriarchal to patriarchal eras. The solar heroes would slay the 'dragons' (we sometimes describe difficult mothers-in-law by that name) and dark powerful goddesses like Medusa and Lilith.

These old stories can describe in a visual way some of the truths about human nature. A simple re-reading of a child's book of Greek myths will make you smile. The similarities to our lives, especially in relationships and in politics, are interestingly not time sensitive but recognisable patterns.
The Celtic myths especially allowed for and revealed that time isn't fixed. The gods and goddesses were able to shapeshift and easily traverse past, present and future.
Look back at your favourite storybook character, fairy tale or myth and view what you see with new eyes. Psychoanalysing everything isn't what this is about, heaven forbid! Seeing how we programme ourselves and then live out some themes in an archetypal story can be valuable when we meet a crisis in our life when a pattern has

repeated and we wrongly call it fate or bad luck or attract mates of similar natures.

LEST WE HAVE FACES

We have the story myth of Psyche and Eros, (mind and love) for example. Eros is the god of love and passion, and Psyche the beautiful daughter of a mortal king who, due to various reasons, ends up about to be sacrificed to the gods to absolve a sin of her father's. Eros very much likes what he sees and scoops her up in the dark to his palace. She is asked to trust him and not look at his face.

One night when he visits her and is sleeping, she fears he might be a monster and lights the oil lamp to see his beautiful face. He awakes, turns away his face and flies away. Oh dear! Then begins her toils to find him again. His jealous mother, Aphrodite, sets her seemingly insurmountable tasks to accomplish, but with the help of the nature kingdom she succeeds and is reunited with her love. Along the way she develops strengths and resourcefulness she didn't have before.

This can be seen as finding one's soul mate through tests of trust, a deepening of knowing oneself, commitment and enlisting help. It can also be seen as the inner journey to unite the higher levels of the masculine and feminine within. There are many forms of love: names we get from the Greeks such as Eros; erotic and passionate love; Agape; compassionate, platonic love.

BEING SEEN AS WE ARE

It is not uncommon to hide our true faces and not be seen as we are. We have to be truly *seen* to love and be loved. In the myth Eros did not want to show his golden face did he? It is also the story/myth of finding ones inner soul, the alchemical union of the inner male and female. Idealising a person can cause suffering and illusion; no one is a god. An important theme to look at.

Spirals and labyrinths run through myths, especially when there is a monster to slay and a beautiful princess to be rewarded with! Theseus and the Minotaur of the Cretan legend summed this up well. By allowing ourselves to explore the twists and turns to meet our shadow side, nicely secreted away, is not easy.
To face it, thus taking its power over us away, leads us to unite with, if not a beautiful princess or prince (!), but with a greater understanding of the balance and marriage of light and dark at the soul level.

Then we have fairy tales of good over bad, and journeys to find (inner) gold. Many stories are wrapped around the theme of following the Sun and the marriage of the Sun and Moon. What shines through is the desire for union or reunion with Self, epitomised by the Sun or the Moon or both, the princess or pot of gold.
These motifs running through myth and storytelling are ingrained in us and ingrained in the journeys of *'god's wanderers',* the planets. There are many films and television series at present making those stories entertaining.

Myths have become standard watching for many of us, and whether in that way or through books, by absorbing the themes we are put back in touch with our inner landscape and characters. We can look at people in the public eye and in our personal lives and see subtle or glaring resemblances as well.

Adolf Hitler drew on Teutonic and Aryan myths to stoke up the collective consciousness of the German nation at his rallies.
Leaders often mirror legendary characters. Even the recent President Donald Trump, stirring up a whirlwind of disruption and rebellion,

back down again and autumn and winter occurred. A simple tale, but maybe an important one of attachment and letting go, of reconciliation and change. There are other themes to this myth but I have chosen this version of it to mirror the importance of the light and shadow in life.

When Pluto and his archetype of death and rebirth comes to call, whether in the charts of nations, as we saw in the last chapter regarding the United States, or in our own life, we can expect change of a deep order, eventually followed by regeneration.

And the stories, known and not so familiar, carry on. Get to know a good storyteller who can relate them well and experience an inner process. I know one or two good ones to call on.

TRAVELLING STORYTELLERS

In times past a storyteller would also be a traveller who stopped at villages and was welcomed for a night. He or she would somehow feel the inner story of the community, its troubles, successes and joys and weave a tale which spoke directly to the villagers and communities' hearts. Things moved, were revealed and healed and forgiven. Quite special. The storyteller held a respected place and role in society and had to have a good memory, as these were done orally and often passed down from one generation to another.

So often we have a memory of an event, convinced it's a correct memory with the details etc. Sometimes we discover that some of the facts in it are inaccurate, and yet we had been so sure our memory was true. As we know, witnesses after an accident or other event can have very different stories of what they had seen. Courts of law are full of this!

However, the oral stories passed on from old which captured the full attention of the listeners tended to stay pure and intact. Maybe it was the way they were told. The art of storytelling can hold the memory and continuity of a group or community or culture and has a binding power.

When we collect old photographs and research our family tree we are giving old stories life and meaning. We draw on the tap root we can obtain nourishment from – the talents to learn about, gratitude for what they built in their lives, some lessons not to be repeated perhaps, and a sense of belonging.

UNIVERSAL PARALLELISM

When stories were placed onto the stars many thousands of years ago, relating to the populace and carried down over the centuries, these stories talked about the rising and setting of the heavenly bodies, the passing of time and, collectively, the themes which described our human condition and stories of cycles in the future. Things which were only discovered by astronomers much later due to modern apparatus were somehow known at a deep level and described in a pictorial way.

HOW DID THEY KNOW THAT?

An example is the Dogon tribe in Mali, West Africa who, when two French anthropologists met them in the 1930's, described from their traditions that the dog star Sirius had a companion star circling it which is invisible to the human eye. This legend had been with them for centuries. 'Sirius B', as it has been named, was not discovered scientifically till 1970. I would recommend the book 'The Sirius Mystery' by Robert Temple as worth reading if the subject interests you, and the inner world's geography we are looking at draws you to dig deeper.

Whilst sceptics could query some of this, what cannot be overlooked is that there were artefacts depicting this going back 400 years, and rituals celebrating both stars had long existed in the tribe. They knew Sirius B had a 50 year orbit around Sirius itself and had huge density. The mind can boggle but, if like the hologram, each part contains the whole, then fact may well be stranger than fiction. We know so much more than the brain and senses think they do. Even on a good day!

I believe there is a universal parallelism between myths, stars and the archetypes (primordial collective patterns in the psyche.)
The more bonded a group is, the more telepathy is present. Nowadays, whilst this is still the case, we also have separated ourselves considerably. It is easier to do everything online, and whilst the world wide web (www) is indeed a web and network, intimacy and communication is of a different nature.

Did you know that in 1995 there were 'just' 23,300 websites. By 1996 that number had increased ten-fold. By the time we reached 2016, there were over a billion. If we type a word into a search engine millions of returns can pop up, depending on the word of course. A lot of information and choices. How much do we need? It is valuable in many ways, and has made learning and writing much easier

providing information at a tap of a key, but where does intuition and finding out for ourselves have a look in?
The art of reflection is looking a bit sad. Yes, it's time saving to Google and the like but, a bit like fast transport, we miss so much along the way.

MYSTERIES

It seems that more and more we hear false news on the media and too much information on what we really don't need to hear. True? It's good that things are exposed sometimes so people don't 'get away with things', but the flip side to this is when every detail of a celebrity or other public figure, especially after their death, is written about. A little bit of mystery and avoidance of over analysis keeps the beauty flowing and reminds us, who didn't know them personally, of what their gifts gave to us. A sense of mystery keeps us intrigued and open to magic and awe.

EXPLORERS AT HEART

With so much being spoon fed to us we can lose contact with the natural instincts we are born with, like a tool getting rusty through lack of care and use. What happens when we are suddenly without the technologies and outer advice we use and have to contact the inner compass and gut feeling?

It can be pleasantly surprising when we become aware that the natural part of us holds the keys.
Any crisis puts us back on ourselves to reorientate and find true north again! In some languages, the word *crisis* holds more than one meaning and character. It can also mean a crossroad and opportunity. Usually, it is only in hindsight that we see the last two variations on the word crisis having their potential positivity.
When did you last realise that?

At critical crossroads in life we can choose to rush them or wait for the signs to change to avoid mishap or being stuck in the middle where everything gets held up. What are signs to look for in our inner and outer landscapes? Do we even notice them? Often many small events and mishaps occur before the big one or the end of the cul de sac. We have warnings. Life does try to help us!

I came across a saying, *"If we don't find time for recreation, sooner or later we will be obliged to find time for illness"*. It's true that other people are not less important than us, but they are not more!

When does the inner light go green for *'go',* and do we take advantage of it even? Our attention span is not always good and we can miss our cues, no matter how bright they are. The more we rush and are not in the moment we lose our valuable tracking device.

Let's revisit our inner geographical landscape.

In the notes page at the end of this chapter, or maybe in a journal, jot down some words or even images and colours of how this inner world of yours is looking. You can do this whenever faced with a challenge, fear or new project. As you see its contours, ingredients and 'weather', sit with it a bit and, as it perhaps starts to feel burdensome or boring, change it! A technique which works well is to look way off in the distance or, if you can't do that, look up at the sky and feel it stretching you out and away from the mind-set you are in. Fill your inner world with that big space and let it swirl around and loosen up the picture you saw before.

TRUSTING YOUR COMPASS

At this point, see yourself in the picture image holding a compass with the gentle rays of the sun shining around it. Choose a form of transport - on foot, in a car, train, boat or plane, (with wings if you like!) - and let the magnetic compass swing its pointer to where it wishes to go, trusting that it and your larger Self know best.

Your intellect isn't involved in this landscape remember. So the inner compass will steer you to where your larger Self wants to express itself happily. It might be true north or not. There is a light within, even in a dark place it is there, and as you feel the Sun around you with the compass in your hands, allow the right insights, contacts, words and circumstances to come to you as you go about your day. You have your apparatus and your kit present, just as you would have if going on a physical expedition with its myriad of happy and tricky situations.

THE HEART AS A BIG CONTINENT

Essentially, the heart is the best compass and following it creates authentic action. It is a big country, maybe a continent, in your inner geography and worth visiting regularly and feeling its beat. Part of sickness is losing our primal beat - a falling out of tune. ***How does that continent within you look? Is it fertile and colourful? Is it***

having a big enough say? And who or what part of governing it?

The drum beat was an essential time keeper, as it always is in a musical piece. The American Indian medicine wheel still exists as an important part of their life.

This 'compass' containing the directions of the elements and north, south, east and west, emphasised the need for balance and whole making. All directions of the compass are valid and can show us the direction home when we have come adrift from our centres. The above exercise of going within, holding your unique compass and allowing it to guide you without analysing it, can come into its own when in a fog, as it will not let you down.

Loneliness, it has been said, is the mismatch between you and aspects of your life – places, jobs, people and ….your authenticity. Only you can change that and it starts with finding true north - yourself! The journey to Self is the most important one we can take, and its geography a fascinating exploration. With curiosity, rather than judgement, it is an adventure of a lifetime and enriches our creativity.

Peter Pan may have said that to die will be an awfully big adventure, and no doubt it would and will be, but being reborn *whilst* in a body has to equal that. By reborn I mean living with awareness, so things and habits don't get stuck. Yes, to be truly curious about life and what is around the corner, discovering what the things and people we encounter are all about is a gift. We can start with that lovely approach at any time. A side bonus is that it keeps us moving in time, being excited about the unknown and magic in life. By example, it encourages others.

The best teachers and other adults around us when we are young have that curiosity, sense of adventure, and seem youthful even if not in their years. They haven't lost that spark, even those whose lives have been traumatic or a slog. We need those individuals, don't we?

Slipping out of the old skins, which are out of their time zones and their relevance to the present *'you',* is true free will, otherwise we are fated by them.

When I started to really understand the importance of the mirror of the planetary cycles, and indeed how nature doesn't like being pot bound, I also realised the unique opportunity those signs give us to be at home with ourselves and to keep reinventing in authentic and growth oriented ways our precious lives and spirit.

Albert Schweitzer once said that, ***"The tragedy of life is what dies within a man while he lives."***

I ask the question: What happens to the unlived out parts of us? By that I don't mean we have to be all things to all people and be talented at everything. Leonardo Da Vinci did his best with that! But where do the unlived parts go and why do they, like actors who have stage fright, stay out in the wings allowing, because nature abhors a vacuum, other people to live them out? A thought to ask the heart and its governor about!

UNLIVED PARTS OF US

Where are those unlived parts lurking in our inner landscape and underworld? Shall we give them an airing? They tend to pop up in the beauty of timing at junctions in our lives when there is a sea change happening.

Something leaves our lives, or enters it; something dissatisfies us and we are on a quest for nourishment of a new kind. What talents, dreams in childhood or teenage years didn't get lived out or were pushed another way by life, by education or our parents – or even

lack of confidence? But what isn't lived out doesn't die; it can go underground, neglected, but it will pop up eventually like the seventh wave, wanting to be seen.
We may not be up to making a career out of it for some reason or other, or just maybe we can. However, we can have a go at it to give it an overdue say, can't we?
I was not good (or so I was told and thus believed) at artistically working with my hands as a youngster. So, educationally I was seriously not encouraged in that direction. I drew to me many people who were though. Because they were, I didn't explore that side of me enough. My choice of course, but an easy option!

My career, as I described earlier, came unexpectedly and walked beside me providing huge scope for meeting people, travelling and learning. With self-employment it is easy to let it drift into spare or recreation time and take over.

Things were missing still, I thought, and I resurrected and found time for my love of singing, jazz in particular. Though it pressed many buttons, I came to enjoy performing that way and even had paid gigs. I gave it a big airing for some years. The timing had come around for that part of me, not fully developed in youth, to literally come on stage. I could have ignored it but it wouldn't let me.

I even had an attempt at sculpture. Having always been a kinaesthetic person I admired that art form. Hard work and very odd shapes in stone emerged under my sore fingers. Knowing I was never going to make any money out of that, and didn't need to, I just had fun sculpting. The same applied to drawing, another no - no when young. I had a brief year of loving sitting and copying nature landmarks or objects in the room. They weren't bad at all, and I realised that because I wasn't attached to being good at it or felt I had to compare it with what others drew, I let myself off the hook and just enjoyed. And, just as significantly, I had chosen to do something outside my comfort zone or talent range. *I had chosen an opportunity to be more than the 'me' I knew well.*

Once, on a rainy afternoon, with a gathering of people I was close to, I got us drawing a stove in the room. They were all in varying degrees technically quite good at drawing.
Because they thought they had to be good, it gave them assorted degrees of worry and self-consciousness. I didn't care as I knew it wasn't 'my thing', and with that freedom produced something definitely a bit quirky but admired.

We can only live one life physically at one go, but, exploring on the edge of things and talents that others are doing fully and maybe better, whilst putting our main energy into our career, our relationships etc, feels very whole-making and freeing.

WHEN THE TIME IS RIGHT

I am using those examples to show how, when the muse speaks, as they say, whether in a highly talented person or in someone of average ability, that when the ***time is just right,*** the promptings will not go away lightly. There is always space and time, though we are so good at finding excuses to pull away from the edge – we get edgy!

On that note, how many scary looking edges and cliffs are in your inner world? Or do you maybe like them?
Doing something extremely new, whether we want to take that opening or are forced into it, is very scary, yet exciting. Yet, strangely, it soon becomes familiar and normal. Children must automatically experience that when embracing new things. Otherwise they would never grow. But many of us when older shy away from opportunities where we might find ourselves vulnerable and thin skinned.
The art of timing lies in knowing that when we are perhaps scared, out of comfort zones, with the unknown beckoning, we can TRUST that inner timing and the invisible hand which guides us. We soon

know if it is right for us by the signs and help that appear, along with the synchronous events which occur.
The more we trust our intuition, not giving up when it is a bit off kilter at first or at times, the more it becomes our friend. If we don't trust ourselves how can we trust others or life's potential opportunities?
Yes, life throws us many curve balls or difficulties, but I have seen many people who have had a relatively easy journey sabotage change and good things.

I have also known and know people who have had horrific backgrounds of abuse and loss who still have the lovely curiosity I mentioned earlier along with an openness and an embracing of love, which is, as the poem Desiderata says, *" As perennial as the grass"*.
Age shouldn't be a deterrent, even when physical limitations occur, but it often is chosen to be so.
Just as we can act ourselves into any role, we can act ourselves into being old!

IN-TUITION

The inner tutors I have been writing about in this chapter I find quite comforting as a thought, don't you? Just make sure they are kind, humorous and firm ones. Inner authority figures can be both critical and/or encouraging. It is up to us to choose who instructs us daily... If it is the inner critic, give it a physique, an appearance and maybe a name. Step back in your mind and objectively look at it.

Then shower it with sunlight and see what it looks like now after the glow of the heart of the Sun changes its veneer. Maybe it looks weak or sad or disappears. There's no rush, especially if you have been carrying this wounded and grumpy character around for most of your life.

Why waste time on inner and outer characters, who either are not prepared to grow, or choose not to show the authentic face of encouragement? In our outer life it seems easier to say goodbye to people like that than the inner one! Sacking - and no redundancy pay for it please - might be timely? See what other image can replace it, more in keeping with your birth right, which is to have a wise and graceful teacher and adviser.

As you respect your rights and self value more, so, with the grace of good timing, you will attract more and more people and circumstances that mirror them. How delicious and what an adventure as we occupy our time slot on planet Earth!

NOTES FOR YOURSELF

Chapter Five

NATURAL DIARISTS: FLOWING GRACEFULLY WITH TIME

"God gave us memories that we can have roses in December."

James Barrie, playwright and novelist

We fill our calendars with events, routine appointments and anniversaries; some of us more than others. We are slotting in with life and are busy.

Have you noticed how there are times when we slide away from this? We didn't plan to, but we slip out of linear time, and yet somehow remember what we need to do without checking! Or we keep a journal and there are lapses of time when we don't write. Either we get lazy or we find it missing our attention in some way.

Our right hemisphere brain that needs a break from the linear and logical is shifting our attention away. We glide with time on memory and instinct, feeling okay if a cancellation or postponement crops up. A gap in time is maybe taking place.

We looked at times in the lunar cycle of the month when it's easier to do and allow this. I will be giving this more attention shortly for rhythmically planning the gestation of a project. We looked at times in our year when it is wise to not push the tide.
Our bodies, from nature, will always let us know.

KAIROS – THE WATERSHED OF TIME

There is a hidden order of reality which guides us and a different type of time which the Greeks, who we get a lot of our modern words from, called *kairos*. It represents quality time and knowing the *right or opportune moment* to surrender or act. Time then becomes indeterminate, allowing shifts and significant happenings.

At a deeper level, it is when time stands still due maybe to a big life change suddenly occurring. Sometimes the magnitude of it is so great that how we live our life irrevocably changes. We are held by life in ways which may appear to others as seamless or just lucky, and, like sliding doors, we are in a different landscape, inwardly handing things over to Life.

The philosophical minds of the ancient Greek era saw this time of kairos as a 'letting god' or the higher self having a guiding rein. We may not have even wanted to continue life for some reason that only the heart knows, and then something bigger steps in!

Time and its opportunities have a louder say. Often in worrying that we will miss the boat, the world will forget us if we take a retreat for a while, or that money won't come in, the pathway track of kairos

and the pathway track of man made time cannot work together. We miss so much of importance when we worry.
I talked about trust earlier. Not gullible trust, but the knowing that we can't control everything and instead letting life and our inner timekeepers have a say. Mistrust is a big breeder of hate down the line, and we don't personally need to add to the huge mistrust in the world at large at present. It's infectious and then we forget how much love and kindness there is as well.

Time can stand still in the gap that exists between regular time ticks. If we allow it, the things around us which we feel we can't handle will then, due to the watershed event, start to fall into place. By not writing any clauses into our agreements with life or expectations (which we often do without even sometimes knowing it) we travel a different way alongside the track of normal clock time.
This is valuable knowledge, and I believe we can experience it without a massive trauma or sea change. It does necessitate getting out of our own way though. Not easy, but certainly possible.

Someone not long ago said to me when I was worried about messing up sending something out over the computer, *"No one's going to die!"* True.

Kairos also meant ***a window of time***, which opens then closes. It needs us to be aware of it otherwise we may miss something quite large. Being big enough to accept it is our choice. It can often be led up to by a series of events and signs from life, noticed or overlooked. The expression 'in God's time' has been around forever, and certainly time, not linked with the timepieces which have become more and more sophisticated and which we form dependency on, has its own importance and magic.
Whatever God's time is, whether we believe or not in a God or higher power, it seems to happen when we least expect it and is important. That kind of *time personality* is more significant in the long term than normal time and will find a way of having its day!

The word 'magic' is very much misunderstood. Yet we use it as an adjective regularly. Maybe magic is just natural laws we haven't general access to, reliant as we are on the brain and five senses - the reducing valve. We call something magical when it surprises and delights us. We don't query the usage of that word in that context so maybe it really does have a place in life.

We looked at chronological 'father time' and how it can eat us up as though it has a mind of its own. Or so it seems as modern life doesn't value rest as much as it might. A busy person, yes, gets a lot done, and is generally admired. But is there a balance in the way we breathe, physically and metaphorically, with our scurrying around? Life will always get on without us, but we act as though the centre won't hold if we don't follow through or fill that slot. Okay, we know all this – do we?

Or are you reading this at a time when it is a timely reminder? There are no random coincidences in life, only meaningful ones.

CLOCKS STOPPING

We use time devices to let us know when we have an appointment or to wake up. Clocks sometimes stop! That is a fact of life, whether the battery has died or we drop a watch or clock and the mechanism breaks. So we fix it or buy a new device. Or for a while we don't. There is a phenomenon worth a look at here. People report that clocks or watches stop at the same time that a charged event occurs. This could be an event that we hear news of later, maybe even a death. And we realise that event had occurred exactly at the *'time the time stopped!'*

Something we rely on in daily life is behaving as though it has a mind. It is as though there are mysteries we cannot comprehend, and I rather like that. The universe and the bigger web around us is full of 'energy tendrils'. The more charged and important the event, the more signals and 'announcements' appear from unlikely places.

Think on this; have you ever noticed that when a clock stops and we don't bother to get it going again, time in a strange way gets suspended? Things get stuck or don't move flowingly. When we put that new battery in things start flowing again. I hadn't myself realised this till a few comments came my way from people who had observed this at work. As an experiment, get out of a drawer a dead battery watch and put a new battery in, or fix a clock which has stopped and see if events, communications and projects get a move on. Especially if the clock is in a focal position in your home or work place this may be more apparent.

Machines mirror and can be affected by our energies, of that I am sure. We have all experienced when frustrated or angry our car, bike or computer playing up. They fall into a synchronous pattern with us. Our electrical circuits are more than we perhaps fully understand and, when we short circuit our emotions, other things around us can do the same. Strange maybe, but, as Shakespeare's Hamlet said, *"There are more things in heaven and earth Horatio than are dreamt of in your philosophy"*.

Never make the mistake, as a wise person once told me, of letting a machine know you are in a hurry!

SYNCHRONICITIES

When we are giving our attention to some matter, things resonating to it spring up all around us. We have all experienced the phone ringing just as we are thinking of a person and it is he or she on the other end of the line. This gets especially odd when we haven't seen that person in a long while. Perhaps we are in an out of the way place, maybe abroad, and around the corner walks someone who lives near to us at home. Generally we forget it quite quickly; it's as though part of us know it's not so abnormal and accepts it after the first surprise. It can be comforting as well to know we have the attention of the invisible field around us.

I am finding as I write this book that time and again an interesting synchronicity occurs. Sometimes I have the radio on in the background. Just the background hum can be helpful, though at other times silence is easier. I am not listening consciously, unless I take a pause and stretch, but I find that occasionally as I am writing a fact or historical reference or something about spirals or a plant that, lo

and behold, the same words or subject are being discussed on the radio. My ears prick up as some of these ideas have been the more obscure things!
I smile and think that, oh well, I am on the right track. Something feels in sync and in tandem with me as I write. Have you known something similar? Undoubtedly.

Perhaps these occurrences mark a natural diary at work. We can plan and fill in calendars as much as we like, but our inner timetable and needs create their own appointments! It would be interesting for you to look at a week in your phone or paper diary calendar and jot, beside the events and meetings there, the other things that naturally sprang up like significant encounters, fortuitous happenings, and insights which perhaps make us change our itineraries.

I love the sychronicities that spring up when we are on the right track, and have even learnt to respect the warning signs and irritants around me which tell me to realign and maybe take a pause. We don't just strain at the seams of our clothes when we put weight on, but also strain our psyches and nervous systems when we overload our minds, emotions and nerves!

SERENDIPITY

The word serendipity was coined in 1754 by a Horace Walpole. He came across a Persian fairy tale called *'The Three Princes of Serendip'.* The princes were always making discoveries, by accident, of things they were not in quest of but turned out to be useful ones! Horace compared this to happenings he had heard of and known, and the word was born. Apparently serendipity, according to a British translation company in 2004, was voted one of the ten hardest words to translate or explain. No surprise there as when time takes us on its own purposeful meanderings, how can logic have its usual say?

In science, it is a common occurrence. Alexander Fleming accidentally discovered penicillin that way in 1928. Percy Spencer, an engineer in the 1940's, discovered and invented the microwave by 'accident'. He worked in a company and was testing a military-grade magnetron and suddenly realised the peanut snack in his pocket had melted. Curious - yes, back to that wonderful word *'curiosity'* - he ran another test with an egg which exploded in his face and then a third test with popcorn. The kitchen microwave oven was born.

I am sure you can think of other examples. The point of mentioning this is that just as we think we are employing time in a certain way or for a certain purpose, it has another agenda - a mind of its own if you like! Our natural diaries are at work.
Yes, time does strange things.

OUR TIME HAS COME

We hear people say that *"my time has come!"* Things in their life are coming together nicely, hard work has been rewarded and they are on 'a roller'. We should be happy when we hear that, as everything has cycles and changes, but bathing in the wonderful feeling of that roller, a bit like riding the wave in style, needs truly appreciating. When the troughs and quiet times occur, we can trust they have their importance too. The well has to fill up and await the next 'up' cycle.

We should never hide our light and, by glowing with that feeling, we encourage others to shine too. Power times, being fully in love with the pulse of being alive and our own beat, are crests of the wave and need celebrating.

LIVING A THOUSAND LIVES

I came across this beautiful piece of writing and wanted to share it here.

Sophie Sabbage's book, "The Cancer Whisperer," is the story of her attitude and journey through a diagnosis of 'incurable' lung cancer and numerous brain tumours. A remarkable woman and a remarkable story of doing things her way! With her kind permission I include these lines:

"... living a thousand lives. I love that. Before cancer, time was thin. I lost it regularly. Whole days would pass by without me making something of them. Other days were packed with busyness, but no presence, no savouring the bounty of a moment.

In crisis time gets fat. It opens layer by layer like a peony. It's similar to that moment when you finally kiss someone you've been aching for and melt into so much tenderness that time stands still and bows.

....anyone of us can be taken out at any moment.... it does put you on notice. It invites you to live a thousand lives in whatever time you are granted, without ever knowing how much time that is."

Thank you for these wise words Sophie!

SEASONS OF OUR LIVES

There is an old saying that the blood changes at the onset of spring and autumn. The 'tides' move our currents. Even in countries where the seasons don't seem to change much, the inner timekeepers we have still know there is a change afoot.
The body and the markets respond as well. Going back to the trader W.D. Gann, whom I mentioned earlier, he made the claim that capital and commodity markets tend to top on or around September 22nd more often than on other dates. Big collapses, bull market highs, gold booms and the like clustered around that date regularly. You can easily check these out. At the autumn equinox, around that date, as the Sun enters the balance sign of Libra, the scales, adjustments and 'swings' occur.

The rising sap of spring reaches its peak and the 'fall' time, half a year on, is a sensitive point for many of our cycles.
A study was done at the department of neuroanatomy at Yale medical school, which discovered that the human nervous system typically undergoes measurable changes during late September. To a lesser extent around the spring equinox in later March too.
In the natural circle of the year, which the 12 signs of the zodiac are linked with, these signs are also linked with nature and the seasons.

Even when reversed in the southern hemisphere, there are three signs for each season. The start of spring, Aries, and the start of autumn, Libra, are when there is equal day and night. Equi - equal and nox - night.

The ongoing controversy of why astrologers specify 12 zodiac signs gets rather tiresome when scientists love to periodically dredge up how many 'signs' there are (there are at least 1,022 constellations, and the zodiac and the constellations are different). Critics overlook the natural calendar which we are heir to and live and breathe. The 12 signs correspond to the four seasons, three signs in each, which our bodies, as nature, are part of.

The number 12 - of course in lunar astrology there are 13 lunar months - is an imprint in our souls and psyches and has run through myth, symbolism, stories and scriptures for aeons. Just as if we place six circles together, they create space for a seventh in the middle, so also 12 circles create space for a thirteenth in the centre.

HARMONY OF THE SPHERES

The zodiac signs we know so well from star columns in newspapers, have a resonance and connection deep within us. They represent nature, archetypes from old and stories we carry within and live out in character /personality roles and the like. The angles between the planets and their ongoing cycles are used more in terms of timing and forecasting.

Like a beautiful symphony, they mirror and help us make sense of growth patterns and change. No wonder the astronomer Kepler talked about the harmony of the spheres. He was convinced that the planets had their sound tones and created their own music as they moved.

Shakespeare also implied this and, in the lines from The Merchant of Venice, he sums it up poetically and insightfully:

"...look how the floor of heaven is thick inlaid with patines of bright gold: There's not the slightest orb which thou behold'st but in his mercy like an angel sings still quiring to the young-eyed cherubim. Such harmony is in immortal souls but, whilst this muddy vesture of decay doth grossly close it in, we cannot hear it."

The seasons herald appointment times with nature. Our inner diaries know these things and want us to readjust and take stock at those junctions. Festivals of the year were always important for acknowledgement of nature's rhythm. We find and are reminded of our place in the bigger picture and Earth's yearly rotation. It doesn't do us any harm to be in the moment and 'turn the corner' with those signposts.

Connecting with the equinoctal and solstice dates, and the cross quarter festivals of Imbolc, Beltane, Lammas and Samhain which fall midpoint between the solstices and equinoxes, and greeting the coming times with gratitude is empowering. It slots us into the 'new' vibration. We can approach this as we would a person, requesting its help in the coming three months for plans. This sets *intent* into motion.

SPACE WITHIN TIME

I like to honour the sacred dark spaces between things we do and say. They are an essential part of our inner natural diaries. In the darkness things germinate, develop and are made clearer. With so much change, unsettledness and technological development and stress around, the volume of inner and outer noise has been turned up and shows no sign of decreasing.

Silence gives intuition a home and release.

In silence and pausing, these noises can subside. The other senses waiting in the wings can indeed be sensed; time is not wasted.

Indeed, it is enhanced and used more wisely with discernment. We don't allow ourselves enough space in life. We hear people say *"I need space,"* especially in relationships where they feel rather suffocated, not least of all by themselves due to not feeling free inside.

In a stage play there are often intervals; a breathing space for actors, for audience and stage set changing. In our own play of life, do we know when to take those?

The original introduction of coffee and tea breaks in the office came about because of the awareness of dips in energy during the day. Nowadays it doesn't always happen, even proper lunch breaks are ignored or not allowed; time is money and all that!

CONSIDER THIS

Many years ago I was given a book by John Stewart Collis, a poet and academic who pioneered the ecology movement, entitled *'Vision Of Glory'*. In it he explained the extraordinary nature of the ordinary. It has always stayed in my mind as indeed some books do with us. In it he writes about the illusion of matter. At school we were taught

that matter is energy vibrating so fast we see it as solid and that the universe is made up of waves and particles which are interchangeable.
What appears to be terra firma is mainly empty; holes if you like. In subatomic physics we learn that the nucleus of the atom is so very small, yet so very heavy. Nearly all of the weight of the atom resides within the nucleus which is so very small. The volume of space kept clear by the electrons is enormously greater than the total volume of the electrons themselves. Collis compared them to the ratio between bullets in a battle field.

Thus the space between the orbit and the nucleus is so large as to justify the comparison of '*six electrons in the atom of carbon being like six wasps in Waterloo station, with a fly in the middle representing the nucleus*'.
James Jeans also talked in his lectures at the Royal Institution, London, of the analogy of eight wasps flying blindly in a cage 1,000 miles long, wide and deep, to a model of the distances of the stars. Collis goes on to say that if we empty the emptiness out of an elephant it would start to shrink to the size of a mouse. If the Empire State Building in New York were to be treated similarly it would lodge comfortably on the head of a pin but would be hard to pick up as it would weigh thousands of tons! How *can* we imagine the

essential hollowness of things? We think of the constellations of the heavens and the uncounted galaxies, yet most of it is space and dark matter. When we think again about the wasp analogy, maybe we can visualise this better.
In the vast sea of energy, only 4% is physical matter and the rest is called dark matter and dark energy.

Our understanding of physics is a moveable feast and the more we know the less we seem to know. Mystery rears its head regularly.
Rupert Sheldrake, the remarkable biologist and scientist, is known for his theory of morphogenetic fields. He talks about form-shaping fields that control the development of animal embryos and the growth of plants, and suggested that these fields have inherent memory. They are a field of energy drawing upon a collective memory and patterns of activity resonating across time and space with subsequent patterns. 'Empty' space is vibrant, a communicator; a resonant energy ocean of potential.

In darkness, communication takes on a different shape. Try having a sensitive conversation with a partner in the velvety darkness and the words and meaning convey themselves in such a way that they are heard more authentically. Barriers can be overcome if both individuals are wanting this. Light can distract and separate.

Darkness can bind. Our intuition, combined with our hearing, is heightened, so choosing the right timing for this can make the difference to an outcome.

DOORS OF PERCEPTION

The brain and five senses act like a reductive valve. This is probably just as well as if all the doors of perception were opened, certainly without due preparation, the overload of stimuli from the unconscious and all the energy fields would be unbearable. Aldous Huxley didn't just write *Brave New World;* he also wrote *Doors of Perception,* a quite remarkable long essay on essentially what it would feel like to open those doors and be exposed to, well, a very different world!

The desire and pull for unity and oneness is hard to establish in our three dimensional world. Beyond that world is the interconnected web and field of perception not known to our senses. These amazing five senses are of course needed to participate practically in everyday life. He wrote about the enlightened visions and experiences of yogis who had trained themselves to be in that world where our normal senses and brain's compartments are bypassed. With a research

investigator, he took some mescaline and proceeded to try to explain what he experienced.
He found that meaning and being were much more interesting than measures and locations or clock time. The objects, flowers, and colours glowed with light. He was reminded of words from visionaries and great artists who described what they were seeing and translating into creative forms.
Their gifts flowed because the reductive valve was wider open and their inspirations were coming from a higher source.

Huxley was describing fragments of this but his experiences also felt overwhelming and at times frightening. Drugs don't match in a healthy way what the yogis and artists can tap into and bring through to this world. Even some of the geniuses whose works inspire us couldn't handle the input without resultant madness and breakdowns. The difference between those portals and landscapes and the ones experienced by people with mental illness or who are on drug trips are, literally, worlds apart in terms of consciousness and danger. Seductive and unstable to the unprepared, or available to access if a spiritual path with balance and meditation and time (no short cuts) is embarked upon. If the 'doors of perception' were cleansed, things would be seen as they truly are.

To live 'in the world' we need to have filters for day to day life even though it is perhaps good to acknowledge there is so much more to this mysterious universe we live in.

We are fortunate to have great writings, art and music to put us in touch with such beauty. The word 'paradise' means beyond division. On Earth we are separate as forms, unless we touch. But the draw to transcend self and be part of something larger pulls us via religion, the arts, lovemaking, or alcohol and drugs, to yearn for merging.

Paradise is a tantalising state, not least because we view it as other worldly. And, like homesickness, it calls us.

If we got so caught up with endlessly looking at a flower or a chair we could get obsessed with the intricate details of it forever. The rest of life would be neglected. Huxley did this for a while in the experiment.

He also reported about a friend's wife who had advanced mental illness and who was obsessive about the intricacies of a piece of material and its vibrating beauty.

MINI-ENLIGHTENMENTS

If, however, we are fortunate in our life to have one or more experiences of being outside time and space (they can come upon us very suddenly), treasure them and their beauty. A sense of sudden happiness where everything is glowing comes upon us for no obvious reason as we go about our day. There comes a glimpse of insight into why we are here which makes total sense, a feeling of heart full grace and love in a situation, a sense of being at one with another person.
All these states show we have entered a doorway for a while from... *"out of the commonplace into the rare,"* as the song, *'Stranger in Paradise'* describes, and returned unharmed and uplifted.

Coming back down or returning to our everyday state of consciousness may not be as painful as from taking chemical substances, but reluctantly we still have to adjust to it as life, as we know it here, takes precedence again.
It needs to as we are going through much change and questioning on Earth, and keeping grounded and in balance are important keywords now.

Yet, glimpses of a hidden order of reality now and then are reminders when we get anxious and close down our capacity to be more than we think we are!

GESTATING OUR PROJECTS AND GOALS

So far here we have been looking at how time's place in our lives can bend and play surprising roles for us. It keeps us on our toes when we get complacent, moving us in ways to do things differently.

We talk about the gestation of things, the gestating of an idea and, of course, the gestation cycle in the womb which leads to birth. Fertility is very much part of nature's dream and purpose. For most women, it is an intrinsic part of life. There are biologically times of the month we are told when conception is more likely and times when it is not.
That doesn't always follow the rule though. Just as babies tend to choose their own time for arrival on life's stage, so maybe their souls have a say in conception also!

Nature knows best and it is not unusual for women to conceive when in the menstruating time of month. The expression, '*trying* for a baby', can get in the way when the urge is on to get pregnant. Just as it is not uncommon to get pregnant when one has given up thinking one will or can.

CONCEPTION AND THE MOON

We looked earlier at the role of the moon's cycles and change. Based on the research and big surveys of a Czech doctor Eugene Jonas, back in the latter half of the last century, information came to light of a fascinating link with the moon's phases. He claimed 97% accuracy when it came to conception times.

This is what he published:

That there was a high accuracy with fertile times when the woman's angular relationship - the phase - between the sun and moon at her own birth, coincides with the same phase in the month when she conceives. So, for example, if there are 90 degrees separating the two luminaries at birth, ideal cosmo-fertility conditions are present when that same phase occurs in any month later in life.

This was tested on about 10,000 women with the high degree of accuracy mentioned. Jonas had originally, after studying astronomy, cosmobiology and sun spot activity, and earning respect in those arenas, come across an old Assyrian Babylonian document saying

that *'Woman is only fertile during a certain phase of the month'*. It didn't say which phase, so he started researching.
Since then there has been increasing evidence for this. On a small scale I have known several friends and quite a few clients who had conceived at the same phase of the moon as when they were born. There is also some evidence for the fact that male children are conceived when the moon is in a fire or air element sign of the zodiac - Aries, Gemini, Leo, Libra, Sagittarius, Aquarius, and girls when the moon is in a water or earth sign - Taurus, Cancer, Virgo, Scorpio, Capricorn, Pisces. The research goes on...
We can laugh at the fact that our ancestors thought the moon herself impregnated women, but maybe the wiser minds of those times understood the correlation between lunar cycles and women's cycles. We have looked earlier at the influence of the moon on life on Earth, so maybe it is no surprise?
On that thought it might be useful to use the phase of the Moon you were born at as good timing to initiate and *conceive* a project or idea. There is so much information out there now regarding cosmobiology that I would encourage you to read up on some.
Jonas and his peers steered clear of horoscopes and fortune telling, as did Dr Percy Seymour, an astronomer, astrophysicist and senior lecturer from England, who risked the ridicule of his peers when he was asked if astrology was rubbish. Instead of immediately saying

that it was, he decided to investigate it. To his surprise, he found interesting correlations between the movements of the planets and life here.

He wrote a book entitled *Astrology: The Evidence of Science,* and more recently *The Scientific basis of Astrology: Tuning to the music of the Planets,* about the link between what is above and what is below. He writes about how the human foetus is affected by the earth's magnetic field and the interactions between that and the planets, and how birth is triggered by those same signals. His ideas about genetics and patterns and cosmic rhythms are also interesting.

I can only touch on these points of research and study but I hope it inspires you to look into it more yourself.

MOON FAMILIES

Let us look at the nine month gestation cycle in relation to 'moon families' of projects, and events. You can use this technique by just following the moon's phases on a calendar of the year.

Moon families was the brain child of Dietrech Pessin, who a couple or so decades ago discovered that the four major phases of the month

of 29 and a half days, could also be played out at nine monthly intervals over a 27 month cycle: two and a quarter years.
In that duration period these phases occur in the same zodiac sign and near the same degree.
So if we start at a new moon date say November 29th 2016 when it is in Scorpio, nine months on there is the waxing quarter moon in Scorpio on 28th August 2017.
Nine months on there will be a Full Moon in Scorpio on May 28th 2018, and finally the waning quarter moon in Scorpio on February 25th 2019, all near the same degree and easy to check on the web, or via an astrology programme or moon diary.

The meaning of the phases of the moon are as they would apply in one month. So, if we take the example of someone opening up a restaurant bar on the New Moon (beginnings and a good time to have a start date whether in intent or action,) we can expect the quarter moon date nine months on to be seeing some change.
From the seed sown, issues then emerge that require attention. Things can go up a gear, and things put into motion nine months before start to demand more attention. At the Full Moon nine months later, and 18 months from the actual start, we can expect to see a culmination and bigger public profile regarding plans and issues. It's maybe a good time for a bigger launch or celebration. Partnership

issues can come to the fore. Sometimes, expansion as well takes place.
Nine months on at the last quarter moon, reviews, maybe closure of certain aspects of it and getting rid of 'dead wood' are on the agenda. Preparing in some way for the new cycle is good to initiate now.

NINE MONTH CYCLES OF GROWTH AND CHANGE - A FAMILY AFFAIR

Even without checking lunar positions, and I appreciate you may not want to do that, you can still work with the gestation cycle of time. If something is coming to a head or there is a difficulty in your life, look back almost exactly nine months and check what was happening then. What got initiated inwardly or outwardly? Maybe even look back 18 months. You can be sure that where you are *now* with the issue, it will evolve in the ongoing nine month cycles ahead. There is a rhythmical background of the cycle from before, and it will play out in the following ones.

Choosing a New Moon to start or incubate an idea, goal or business, is a powerful energy time. It can be wise to allow a few days to implement fully though. The seed needs to get settled!

I have worked with quite a few clients using this technique of the moon families, and it really works out. With the confidence born from this, it has encouraged them to deliberately use it as a spreadsheet to plan ahead. I have looked back at these cycles for myself and seen them beautifully unfold.

Events on the world stage also follow suit. You might want to keep up with the referendum cycle here in the UK from June 23rd 2016 or the win of President Donald Trump, and watch the next few nine month dates.

From the start of the event itself (even if it wasn't on a specific phase) to the next date, nine months on, see what has evolved. Then travel another nine months on, and see what is culminating in some way, and then finally another nine months and see what is ready for release, may get rewards in some way or need re checking or rectifying.

Interestingly, as it is very much topical at the time of writing, the result of the American presidential election came on the day after the waxing quarter moon. Energy was up and feisty at that stage from seeds planted nine months before – last February 2016. Nine months on from November 8th we reach next August 7th 2017 at its full moon stage in the gestation cycle of two and a quarter years. We can expect larger than life revelations and exposure, whether good or bad, light being shed on the situation, cards on table and 'partnership' issues to address if relevant. Stress and chaos can be apparent if things aren't in good shape.

Two weeks later, when the total solar eclipse's path in Leo traverses the USA, its path moving from the west coast and finishing through the east and Washington DC on 21st August, significant events regarding leaders might occur.

I have gone into this in some depth because whether you want to keep tabs on this kind of activity or not, it does reveal patterns and the tides of change and development.

Gestation cycles, whether in the short cycle of the month from one phase of the moon till it comes round again, or in the larger picture of 'events families' over two and a half years really work. It isn't so much what *will* happen as much as *when*, and the type of energy- beginning, growth, expansion, rectifying or replanning. It is useful for our businesses as well to have this tool box.

Thank you Dietrich for your research and thank you also Frank Clifford of the London School of Astrology for the chats about Moon Families. There is much more of interest to this work but I have condensed some of the material to fit into the purpose of this theme of inner timekeepers and their diaries.

In a strange but lovely way, working with our inner lunar cycles, whether in our personal life or in the life of our business and indeed the life of our children, keeps us on track with the waxing and waning of the vitality and purpose of the important things in our lives.

Whatever ways in which we choose to track our timing and progress, apart from outer appointment calendars, remember that ***starting points*** set the future cycles. How we start, the factors surrounding it, how balanced we are as we initiate it and what our intent is, all set the trend and rhythm. Every business and project needs cyclical awareness. We wouldn't, if we were a farmer, pull on the roots of crops and plants to make them grow ...would we?

We can sense, just like the phases of the Moon, a time to start or re brand, a time to get action going and to build up, a time to go public more, showing off the project's benefits in some way, and a time to recharge, reassess, re-plan and check details. Our body is the best instrument for our intuition and natural diaries. It will always tell us what we need, and how well or not we are digesting life.

VALUES

Until we value ourselves we won't value time. Whatever we place value on will guide our choices and how we spend time. It is that simple. ‘Quality time’ is a much used phrase nowadays, but its importance lies in the appreciation of being in touch with the promptings we get when we quieten the inner noise. Space and time truly are a continuum when they allow each other room to breathe and be valued!

Running out of space and or time are expressions we regularly hear. There is always room for space and time however when we form a good relationship with them inside ourselves, allowing them to be friends with us as we go about our day. Checking in with them from time to time will provide the right answers. They won't let us down and we can start to rely on them that way with gratitude.

NOTES FOR YOURSELF

Chapter Six

GOOD DECISIONS TO EMPOWER YOURSELF

"Ring the bells that still can ring, forget your perfect offering. There is a crack, a crack in everything; that's how the light gets in."

Leonard Cohen, poet and singer/songwriter.

In the previous chapters we have had a good look at how we can make life more simple and effective for ourselves by understanding timing in all its remarkable forms and places.

We looked at how nature around us, geometrical forms, planetary cycles and numbers, can assist us to make sense of all that we take for granted when we either think we are in line with time or hopelessly lost in it. Or something in between. We looked at the importance of trusting ourselves and being our own teacher and helper when outer signals seem to let us down.

How can we distinguish between the movements of the inner timekeepers akin to our souls, and mere impulsive actions? They are not separate countries, though the landscapes are different, as we are discovering in this book.

Why not check into that inner landscape when you are not sure of when to act? Is it encouraging you to move forward, or to wait?

Remember the word *smog*? If you see and feel smog around you dragging your beautiful senses down, bin the words *should, must, ought to, got to.*

MINDERS

Life is full of reminders; the things that look after us, whether critically or gently. That is what minders do! If our inner authority is healthy then the minders will be healthy too, providing an unwavering support without pressure; if they are harsh and spiky then maybe, just maybe, they have an agenda with themselves more than with us. In either case, they wake us up to be aware of where we are in time and our choices.

So, what are good decisions? It seems sensible to make them but, I wonder, do we make them so things are perfect? Is it that we can feel safe in having proven to ourselves and others that we are on the right track and our life is in good shape? How much responsibility is tied up with them? How much angst and fretting?
Take a moment to think when was the last good, really good decision you made? Is the feeling still with you? Can it enforce the next one? Or did you find you didn't actually make a decision consciously, but you were suddenly living it out and wondering what process took you there? The signs were all there, well most of the time anyway, that a process was under way. In modern physics the idea that the universe is full of processes and consciousness makes sense when we apply it to how we grow and expand.

GOOD DECISIONS REQUIRE RIGHT TIMING

More than we are doers we are deciders, are we not? Intention is the key so we have a good starting point, whether we announce that out loud or within ourselves. The arrow finds it mark. No matter how much we know, tell others or read about this, it is so easy to take decisions too carelessly or impulsively which will vibrate down the line, causing ripples.

When we make a decision which comes from the heart, even in a mundane or very practical situation, it can feel like another self is living and walking besides us. Can you strengthen that sense? It is a part of us, make no mistake, but it is a more aware and wiser part, less conditioned by our backgrounds and all the 'overcoats' we collect around our minds and emotions. The more we recognise it and 'intend' its presence, the more it becomes available to walk with.

We looked earlier at certain planetary and seasonal cycles. There are umpteen more cycles, but just understanding and cooperating with the few spreads the word, so to speak! It then becomes easier and easier to feel the inner signals of our tides changing and to go with their flow.

Even when we are on deadlines and extremely busy with work, duties and timetables, we can understand the need for finding moments of inner space and take that time out for appreciating the beauty around us. We can replenish the roots within us whether literally with healthy food and water or feeding the mind, and, just as importantly, filling that created gap with humour. We can watch the world around us as we breathe deeply and take that shift back into what we are being busy at.

THE VALUE OF BACKWARD MOVEMENT

From plenty of people I hear the comment that they have heard Mercury is about to go retrograde, or it is causing hiccups and delays. We seem to get quite attached to that three week cycle which happens three, sometimes four times a year. It is one of the astronomical phenomena astrologers work with for timing advice, and has its place amongst linear time and calendars.

People who aren't technically au fait with the subject, get access to it via internet comments and the like, so it is becoming common parlance. That is why I thought I would mention it here.

Diaries which have information on the planets contain it for the year ahead, but reading an ephemeris and its symbols demands learning it. So, as long as you are sure of the accuracy of its source, you can check online when the next 'dreaded three week cycle' occurs! The next one starts on April 10th 2017 concluding May 4th 2017. Then we have August 13th to September 5th, followed by December 3rd to 23rd. Always allow a good week or so before and after for full adjustment.

The dates when it is 'stationary' at the commencement and the end are especially sensitive ones, and maybe it is timely to literally go on standstill. This is not always possible of course, but if you can plan around those times with choice and discernment it is helpful to do so. A little knowledge can be, if not dangerous maybe, then at least misleading, so, bearing in mind we need to take all factors into account when putting a label on the effect of a planetary cycle, I will mention here the importance of Mr or Mrs Retrograde.

The prefix *'re'* is the key here. Placing it before words, actions, thoughts, has its importance in how we move forward afterwards when trickster Mercury goes *'direct'*. Moving slowly forward, it then gathers up speed. The words quicksilver mind and mercurial are in our vocabulary. It has a quick orbit compared to the other planets, and in myth, which is always a good mirror, he was the messenger between the gods, humans and the underworld. We like to think we are going forward, don't we? And it is Mercury's function to aid how we think, learn and adapt, which includes re-training, re-editing and re-formulating ideas, thoughts and decisions.

OTHER LANGUAGES

In a birth chart, Mercury shows exactly in what ways we learn best. Are we more analytical, a fast learner, pragmatist, a paced or a visual thinker? An early or late developer? Some of us are of course born with Mercury retrograde, being bestowed with an ability to review well, retrace steps and use the right brain hemisphere well.

Language can be understood differently, with music and other forms of communication holding importance. Sometimes there is difficulty fitting into normal education and teaching methods due to the different mindsets.

For all of us though we do experience its effects during the year. As it slows in relation to the Earth's orbit, thus appearing to retrace degrees of the zodiac, we have the opportunity, *yes, opportunity,* to review what we are doing. I know of companies and businesses who take this quite seriously. Mercury makes a move and so do we. The game of cosmic chess is on!

The universe, in wanting to be noticed, does not wish us to push forward without some rest, reflection or rectification. Our minds are wanting to think differently during these three weeks and even the week or so either side. It is not unusual to have déjà vu experiences and returns of ideas, opportunities and missing objects. All these facts you can find easily on line. Yes, machines play up, travel plans can be chaotic or delayed, and cancellations not uncommon. We get a growing sense we need to backup things and our online data better, and MOTS are useful or forced on us.

This usually comes along at the right time, even if we don't think so. If we are not listening to our inner timing and in-tuition, we can be heading for problems. By being seemingly put on hold in a mysterious way by the cosmic clocks, we can see just where there are cracks and oversights. Maybe, literally, the timing hasn't been right to push ahead.

It's so hard to see this when we think we are on track. Often we *are* on track and we don't experience problems, but it is still worth revisiting ideas, plans and the communications with other people which are part of the processes we are in. It's too easy during that time to have misunderstandings, overlook details and mess up appointment timings. So... double checking and reading fine print on agreements and contracts are invaluable.

RETURNS OF SIGNIFICANCE

When Mercury goes direct, watch that date as it might be timely for important, maybe lasting, connections; the Mercury principle loves connecting the dots. During its retrograde patch one can meet unusual folk and reunite with people we have not seen for a while. With the latter, either we feel that urge to reconnect or it comes out of the blue. I have found it to be the case more than once that when I have visited a country and not intended to return there, that I actually did. It just turned up again! Look for that in your own life.

The reason I wanted to go into some detail on this subject was partly because people have asked me to and partly because it can be significant in good decision making. Sometimes decisions get changed after Mercury has gone direct, so be discerning of what you implement in those three weeks.

It isn't that it is bad luck, or this thing called fate, but the conditions weren't as fixed and in balance, or other people weren't, when we decided on something. Again, reflection, taking a bit of time out and rechecking, are good tools with this short but important cycle. Even waiting can be timely.

In martial arts, allowing the 'other' the first move can be a winning tactic. Stepping aside so the person instead of hitting us goes flying past is easier said than done but the principle applies.

It's no good just to look gloomy and say, *"When will it be over?"* It has its richness and the time is right. With discernment and honouring time in this way, plus having the advantage of knowing the time frame, which is always good news, we can empower our lives and business so much more effectively.

We have all experienced delays and cancellations which beautifully worked to our advantage and gain. When did you last find that?

THE WISDOM OF NON-DOING

Especially when we are tired and yet feel we cannot let someone down and cancel, we find the other person cancels or the event we

were going to gets postponed. Synchronicity is at work and energy is flowing back and forth. When we de-magnetise in some way, the universe responds like sympathetic magic!
On that note of not wanting to do something, let's look briefly at how we can avoid mismatching ourselves with appointments and *'me'* time.

There is no easy answer here; we are not able to foresee how we might be feeling or what mood and energy level will be present. Think on this though; we can be pretty sure that when we are having a lonely patch, thinking the world has forgotten us and our diaries look empty socially, instinctively many of us find things to put in the latter which provides a temporary feeling of being filled up.

When the time comes around, what happens quite often is that the well has filled up and, rather than being in a quiet zone, we are busy enough and we really could do without the 'not thought out' date in the diary we had, in neediness, inserted.
When we have empty times it could be wise to just be with them and wait for the tide to turn. It's the same when we find we have a sudden cancellation, and we want to fill that hour or even day or evening slot with another activity. Sometimes that works, but *'not doing'* and just *'being'* can awaken insights we might not have had otherwise.

We burn ourselves out easily by not knowing our limits or by not listening to our bodies' and minds' pleas. We have glorious free will to do the opposite of what our inner timekeepers want for us! But is it so glorious.

I mentioned in previous chapters some times of the year when it is good to retreat a while. Examples are in the month before our birthday, the month opposite to the one when we were born, the moon when it is in the opposite phase to when we were born. If you know your time of birth, which shows the ascending or rising sign at birth (your persona and face to the world,) the month when the sun is in the zodiac sign before that needs to be quieter. This is to name a few windows of time.

Perhaps what is most important lies in the acknowledgement that the inner tides need to ebb as well as flow, and to watch out for the warning signs outside us as well as on the inside. At the astronomical points I mentioned this becomes even more important.

RE-CREATION TIME

Albert Einstein once said that, *"Creativity is intelligence having fun"*.

The artist Pablo Picasso remarked that, *"Every child is an artist. The problem is how to remain an artist once he grows up"*.

Another catch phrase, 'taking time out', or having an 'away day', allows us to regroup our energies and step outside our normal rhythm and routine. Sleep doesn't always refresh us, but time out can. This is where we grow gracefully with time.

Have you noticed in your own life that on the occasions you finish a working day feeling tired, if you then, instead of being a couch potato or just falling into bed (and yes, they do have their place too), get creative with something which injects passion, you find you have energy? Real dogged tiredness is something different, but when the tiredness stems from the routine, maybe boredom of the day and irritants which have cropped up, along with maybe travel hiccups and the like, the shifting of gear changes us.

Whether by enjoying creative ventures, a hobby, art, or a discussion where imagination or stimulus is injected, renewed energy and alertness are surprisingly present.

The time we spend doing those lovely things has its own life; we recreate our day in a new form.

Recreation or a recreation ground is associated with play, h and games. The prefix're' (again!) suggests we are revisiting or revitalising ourselves. Creation is activity and it links us with the original Creation.

Think on this: If the Creator gave us life, then surely when we are being creative that is when we are most alive? Being creative brings us back to source with the urge to emulate in the spirit of creativity that feeling and joy of being alive. It has been said that when we are being creative there is joy, and when we are joyful that is when it is easy to feel and be creative! Even in the words we speak we are more giving and warm when we feel joy.

It is sad that when the inner critic or outer one truncates this impulse, the natural inner creator becomes like a shrivelled plant, and the world looks and becomes a little greyer. Remember the visualisation I wrote about earlier. The one which helps dissolve the inner critic and as a result allows us, with the law of resonance, to attract healthy advisers in the outside world? This is a really good step to allow the child in us to just have fun with creativity. We are valuing time.

With the first creation stories which abound from many traditions, it was thought that life came out of a void, and the Sun and Moon, followed by the stars, were the first to be created. They took their places!

In the first chapter of the Bible, Genesis, it is written:
'Let there be lights to separate the day from the night. And let them be for signs and for seasons and for days and years. And let them be lights in the firmament of the heavens to give light upon the Earth'.

CLEARING HOUSES: THE ECLIPSES IN OUR LIVES

Eclipses were seen as omens of endings. The darkening of a heavenly body didn't auger well to those ancient eyes. No surprise then that when the Sun completely darkened over at a total solar eclipse people thought the end had come. They noted that eclipses coincided with the demise of leaders, and with earthquakes. Not at all uncommon still to this day.

It makes interesting reading to see how often endings coincide with eclipses. We can see them as the movers and shakers and wild cards which appear in the year. *'Leiplein' to* leave, and *'ekleipsis' from* the Greek meaning to forsake, to abandon, are translations of the word eclipse.

We tend to feel extra tired around an eclipse date. Our energy feels severely depleted and we notice changes in our life path. Solar eclipses, in particular, when the Moon crosses the face of the Sun and is in a line with the Earth, can indicate a clearing, preceded by a bringing up of the past in some way, whether in the mind and emotions or via events from the past rearing their heads.
As a point of interest, eclipses on ones birthday herald a significant year ahead, and bring the message to move forward and turn a big corner. Full Moons do the same to a lesser extent. They bring to attention what is ready for soul growth and, in hindsight, can be looked back on as a year of major shift.

Another person's needs can eclipse our own. Care takers who look after ill or dependent people find that, when attention is given totally to the patient, the carer's needs can get overlooked, even quite often by themselves.
So, at any eclipse in the year, it might be timely to see what is being eclipsed in your life by other things.
It might also be good timing to decide to separate from something for a while to get a fresh perspective. At the solar eclipse, a super New Moon time, the Sun, being the consciousness of the *now*, has its light blocked by the Moon, providing a window of opportunity to have

some kind of realisation about what is running us and has outlived its time and purpose. Endings and beginnings are common.

It is not unusual for political upheavals to occur, and figure heads to topple in some manner. What needs to leave - *'leiplein,'* - leaves, making way for the new.

With the lunar eclipse (a super Full Moon) the Moon passes through the shadow of the Earth. We have an opportunity then to make a move into the future; a crossroad is reached in our psyches.

These eclipses come as a pair! Two weeks separate them in time and we can witness and feel the movement of change and of cause and effect during that time. Watch what happens at the first eclipse date and observe the process leading to the second. There will be a connection. Nothing is settled in that time, so wisdom and instinct are the major players. It is good timing not to start too many big enterprises then.

This isn't day to day decision making. Eclipses cast a deep shadow for many months ahead. Where they aspect our birth charts and where they connect with the grid of countries, we can see in advance where they will leave their mark in the way of events, endings and beginnings.

CRACKS IN TIME

I headed this chapter with a quote from a song, *Anthem* by Leonard Cohen. Many of his lyrics contained prophetic statements, but I think his quote about the beauty of cracks in everything, is his wisest and most important.

Cracks are where the light gets in. We need little cracks in our nervous system to ease the possibility of a big one; too much self control gives rise to panic, and eventual cracks in the woodwork of our lives. The words panic, pandemic and pandemonium stem from the god of ecology and nature, Pan, who represented the primal, wilder, instinctual part of our psyche.

When we are too ordered and have a need to be 'right', panic can begin to set in. The resultant cracks let light in to crevices that have only seen the dark of fear. Fear and control can be seen as two sides of the same coin.

I talked about this in an earlier chapter and, in a world now where there is so much fear resulting in more boundaries and suspicion, extremes develop. Extremes are by nature rigid and countenance no real discussion. Something has to give, with both sides being heard. That is when cracks have their say.

FORGET YOUR PERFECT OFFERING

There is a lovely story from China of a man who every day carried his two water pots, one on either side of his shoulders, to the house of his master. He noticed after a while that one of the pots was leaking water. It had a crack in it. The pot itself was very upset that it was so flawed and causing the poor man extra work by having to make more trips.

The man smiled and said, ***"Haven't you noticed that the plants and flowers on your side of the path are so much more alive and flourishing than the ones on the other side of the path? It is because of the water you are giving them daily. There is no mistake. And my journey everyday is made so much more enjoyable because of their beauty and freshness. Thank you."***

Forget your perfect offering, as the song said!

Good decisions are intrinsically tied up with the cracks that appear in our lives when our timing seems too ordered and perfectly planned. So what are good decisions? What is their goal and who do they serve? What is good now may not be so in a few months; we can only base them on the facts and choices available to us at a particular time.

Do they make us feel at ease once we have made them? Do we feel, like nature does, that there will be growth which will resonate into the future through some kind of morphogenetic field? Did that decision have a path with a heart?

A litany of small decisions escalates into bigger ones. They empower us or they diminish us. The art of timing isn't just about the factors I have discussed between these pages. The picture I have been weaving of the rich tapestry we are part of allows us to trust better the messages we get which surround us.

In nature, geometrical forms, the planets in their courses, and numbers such as the Fibonacci series which run through organic and inanimate form, are there to admire and to be reminders of the knowledge that we really can be the captain and steerer of our timing.

CHALLENGES ARE OPPORTUNITIES

Once we trust in our steering capacity we have then caught an awareness that won't leave us. It clicks into place and stays. Just knowing we are beings of cycles and timing makes it easier to seize the moment and stay true to ourselves.

And there's the rub, as they say. When a challenge rears its head, buttons are pressed in us we didn't even know we had. Timing, response and decisions can lose their moorings.

The bigger the challenge the more important it is we greet it as an opportunity to grow and be tender with. Reacting in aggressive, fearful and defensive ways will short circuit our inner network of skills and harm our intuition. Our 'sailing ship' has been overrun with pirates! Untangling the knots and nets and re-charting our course takes time.

It helps to treat something big like we would something small. There is always a solution, I believe, and taking things bite size helps. It is easy to be overwhelmed by the unknown, which a challenge often is, so jumping headlong into the problem without the right tools and kit rarely works.

Then, in a relaxed state the magic starts to happen. Remember serendipity? We intend a solution, let it go and await the connections and unexpected happenings. Handing it over to the larger Self, that part of ourself that walks invisibly alongside, is a good move. At times like this it can emerge through the crack where the light is now getting in due to our being more vulnerable and less fixed in our mindset. We are open to serendipitous and unexpected chances and solutions.

Some of us want and desire challenges. It feeds us and makes us feel alive. They *are* our opportunities. Others find them difficult and burdensome and want someone else to deal with them. Whichever the case, we still need to nourish the starting point of the potential opportunity that has come our way. Treating it like a companion is an imaginative, yet strangely effective ploy.

We know when a good decision empowers us. At that point, it is so comfortable it takes on a life of its own, without the glitches and holdups poorer ones can produce. It is different to just a good idea that pops up. Being decisive has a clarity and strength of its own, and it is our authenticity which makes or breaks its success. A good decision is often a quiet communicator which holds our hand as the outer noise recedes.

A GOOD JOURNEY

Trusting our inner compass when diverse opinions and advice are rife, is a test. It is also a huge step forward to finding the way home to a larger part of ourselves which has been waiting in the wings.

The more our inner and outer lives, our inner and outer natures, get closer together in harmony, the more likely we are to flow with timely and positive decisions.
What is the binding force between those worlds, the world within the atom and the worlds within our solar system? Do you feel it?
The law of attraction will always shine, between the visible and invisible, between people and between ideas.

We hear and read that the global electro magnetism, the Schumann Resonance, has speeded up in the past few years. Its frequency of 7.8 Hz has hovered there for a long time with small alterations. It has upped its game now. Not just alpha and theta energies, which are in tune with our brains, but beta ones are making us more alert. The 7.8 measurement has been likened to Mother Earth's heart beat. It has a rhythm we are comfortable with.

The monitoring of it has shown sudden spiking of movement in that range into faster beta ones. These can cause dizziness, anxiety and tiredness. As we try to adapt to that new range (and anything fresh to adapt to is a bit scary), new information and awakenings happen. As part of the Earth and its cycles, we are heir to its changes, especially with the magnetic field. Don't rush as much as you did. Settle into this new field as you would a new home.

AWAKENING

To be in time and to turn challenges into opportunities we have to be present fully as nature and the cosmos are. We are *just* as capable of using our antennas to deal with a crisis or cul de sac.
We have looked at ways to do that, but the most important thing to bear in mind is to accept that the challenge is there; it is a living entity just as we are. Avoiding being too cerebral regarding our handling of it, and instead coming from the part of us which is linked with nature's cycles, we start to recognise the way through the maze.

The heroes of old needed to, and perhaps the mark of a hero is to go that extra distance and to hold on that bit longer when others don't. Read the story of Gilgamesh, as a good example of trials, gaining knowledge and returning home with that wisdom.
Not forgetting of course that the wisdom in knowing the time is sometimes right to let go is the art of discernment. We know when and if that time comes; it's only pride and stubbornness which prevent us cooperating.
What would ***love*** do, life asks of us? It is the most powerful force we have and has the greatest capacity and willingness to grow and learn.

Maybe the universal intelligence is a great mind at work moving towards love, and we have the opportunity to bring it back to source as a gift once we have understood it? I like to think that is so

Physics and consciousness may not be so far removed from each other. It seems to be so when we hear that the consciousness of the observer plays a significant part in a scientific experiment. Time and space are ***KNOWN*** at a deep and intimate level to our cells, minds and inner path trackers.

Our ability to time our actions and life path, once allowed some freedom to breathe, draws us closer to the beautiful cycles and purpose we observe every day in the natural world around us.

They become part of us and we feel a part of the tapestry of life... that inherent harmony can go a long way to healing divides and extremes. If indeed, *'life is something that happens to us when we are making other plans',* maybe we can choose to have a greater say in that happening as much as the clock and calendar time slots we revere so much.

When we are planning things, intuition steps up and kindly reminds us to pace ourselves, hold back and then, at the right moment, move forward. This rarely fails, though to other people it may appear we are being reticent. A message within about our timing is always there if we give it space to present itself!

This quote from the physicist John Wheeler comes to my mind as a vision to treasure as we walk our days and years. Also when we wonder why we are here and what our time here is all about:

"To my mind, there must be at the bottom of it all an utterly simple idea. And to me, that idea when we finally discover it, will be so compelling, so inevitable, so beautiful, that we will say to each other... oh, how could it have been otherwise?"

Timing embraces so many things: nature, poetry, music, physics, astronomy, astrology and biology. It runs through the veins of life. It is a pulse and tidal rhythm mirrored in the things around us. That same pulse is ours for utilizing when it comes to the major decisions and the desire to flow with our day.

Glimpses of their common language which we all share are ours for catching.

I hope the glimpses and threads I have shared here will act as keys to unlock some of your inner timekeepers, reminding you of how much you actually know at heart, where it matters and when it matters.

Time is on your side

NOTES FOR YOURSELF

About The Author

Ysanne Lewis has been happily working with timing people's cycles and decision making for over 38 years.
After a background in and a love for the performing arts, she developed an interest in maps of consciousness like astrology and numerology, and their link with psychology and cycles of growth in our lives. Self-employment drew her, and in 1979 she took up the tools of her trade; helping people and businesses with their timing and challenges. Over the years, she has been in demand in the UK and abroad for talks, seminars and individual consultations.

To keep her work moving and interesting for herself, she expanded it into many fields of life including drama, working with theatre companies here, in Iceland, the west coast of America and Finland. Other areas include finance, colour psychology and the health field.
Her love of travel saw her visiting, by invitation, places as far flung as Oman, Hong Kong, USA, South Africa and Denmark, as well as other European countries, and she considers it a privilege to bring and share her skills there.
She has written for many magazines, been an entertaining and informative speaker and a panellist. She has been interviewed by the media, and hosts regular shows as The Timing Host on Radio Works

World. Do contact her if you would like to be a guest on her show! She sees herself as an explorer of what makes us all tick and want to grow, and loves generating enthusiasm through her work for life's rich tapestry of new discoveries and possibilities.
With an early love of stories and myths, she found a receptive home for them in the language of the stars, astrology, and enjoys helping people explore their own stories, heritage and patterns in that way.
Ysanne has found her career a good friend which has given her so much opportunity to work freely in her own time and way, to enjoy public speaking and meet fascinating people with their life stories.
She has co-authored a book in CD format, *To Touch The Face Of The Stars',* with words, music and visualisations. This recording enables us to meet our inner stories and the planets which are alive as characters within us. *The Time Catcher* has been a dream of hers to write for years. It was launched at the Authors' Awards at the Baftas, London, December 2016.

Her aim is to play her part in honouring the beautiful symmetry and intelligence present in the interconnection of what is above and what is below, on earth as it is in the heavens.

Ysanne lives in Surrey, England and would love to hear about your own insights on timing. Contact her at info@ysanne.com.

Testimonials

"Ysanne has amazed me time and again with her 'spot on' readings. The most recent involved a reading regarding a prospective career change. I had been offered a job in a completely different field and was very excited about making a change. However I would be leaving a 30 year career and wanted to be sure that I had fully considered all angles of this decision. Ysanne provided valuable guidance concerning this change. When she asked me when I thought I might start this new job, I told her it would be at the end of July. She hesitated as she consulted her charts and then told me that she felt it would be closer to the end of August. Here's the most amazing thing: I started my new job on August 31st!

Ysanne has become a respected guide in my life. I won't make a major move without consulting her first!"

Michelle Benedict-Jones*, Vice President of Development and Community Engagement, NY, USA.*

Working together to build and sustain hunger free communities throughout the Southern Tier.

"Talking with Ysanne was like being reassured that everything I'm working towards will come to fruition. Instead of trying to predict my future, which I'd find uncomfortable, she focused on my energy flow and explained when some activities will seem easier to implement than others. Ysanne helped me put things into perspective for 2017. Watch this space...!"

Jess Baker *CPsychol, Chartered Psychologist*

"A thorough and professional reader of the present, the past and the future. Practical, spiritual and totally inspiring. I cannot recommend her enough."

Juliet Donovan, *Barrister, Criminal Law, UK*

"Ysanne has an uncanny knack of suggesting when certain leads and opportunities might open up, and a helpful way of suggesting when a particular action might be timely and most effective. It can save on a lot of wasted time, energy and frustration!"

Philip Littlehales, *Real Estate Consultant, London*